THE SECRET LANGUAGE OF DARKNESS

SOUL LIGHT TRANSMISSIONS FROM THE SHADOW

DENISE JARVIE

Copyright © 2024 Denise Jarvie
Artwork Copyright © 2024 Daniel B. Holeman

All rights reserved. Other than for personal use, no part of these cards or this book may be reproduced in any way, in whole or part, without the written consent of the copyright holder or publisher. This publication is intended for spiritual and emotional guidance only. The content is not intended to replace medical assistance or treatment. The views and opinions expressed by the author, both within and outside of this publication, do not necessarily reflect the views of the publisher.

Published by Blue Angel Publishing®
10 Trafford Court, Wheelers Hill,
Victoria, Australia 3150
E-mail: info@blueangelonline.com
Website: www.blueangelonline.com

Guidebook and card messages by Denise Jarvie
Card artwork by Daniel B. Holeman

Edited by Leela J. Williams and Peter Loupelis

Blue Angel is a registered trademark of Blue Angel Gallery Pty Ltd.

ISBN: 978-1-922574-16-9

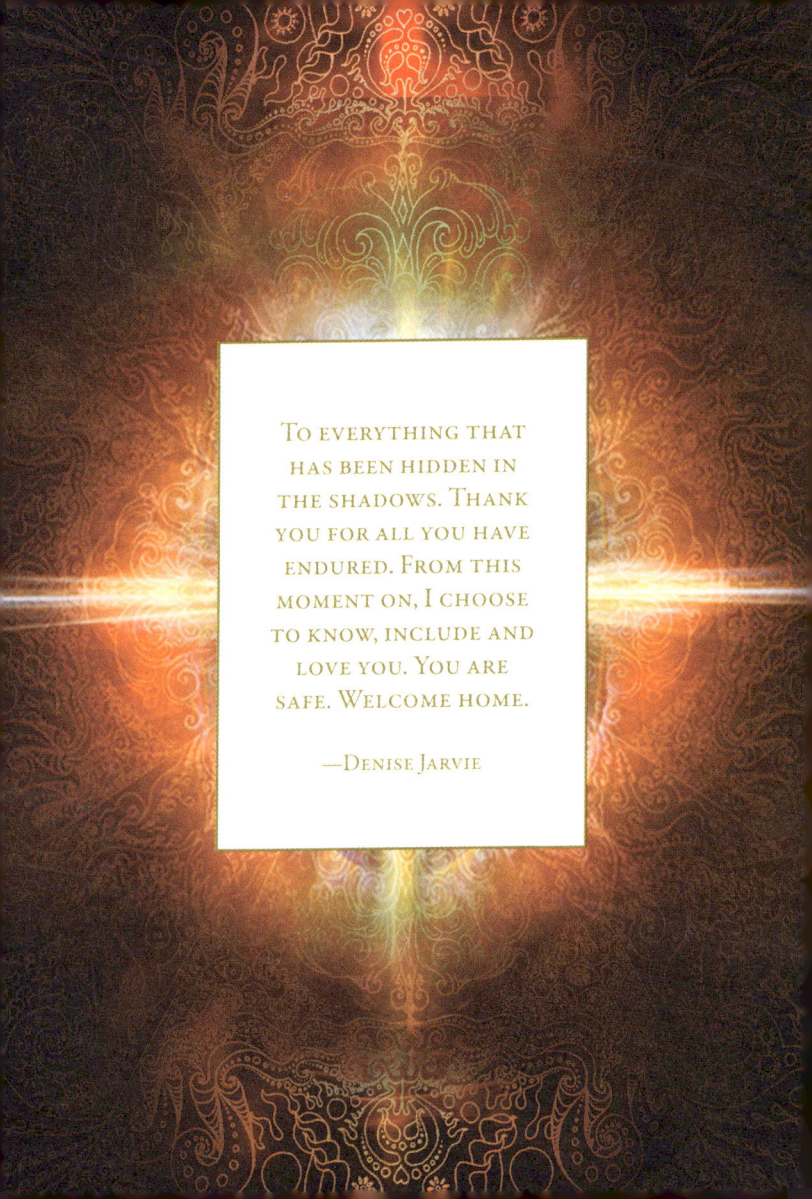

To everything that has been hidden in the shadows. Thank you for all you have endured. From this moment on, I choose to know, include and love you. You are safe. Welcome home.

—Denise Jarvie

> We each need
> to become our own hero.
>
> — Debbie Ford

ACKNOWLEDGEMENTS

THANK YOU to my shadow for storing my darkness until I was ready to embrace it.

Korē, thank you for your persistence in integrating the below world into the above world and beyond.

Thank you to the most talented and hardworking team at Blue Angel Publishing.

Thank you to Richard for your patience and support.

Thank you to Daniel Holeman for his light-filled art, which brings enlightenment and healing to darkness.

Thank you to Carl Jung, Saint John of the Cross, Debbie Ford, Thomas Moore and all who dedicate their lives to understanding the unknown for the advancement of humanity and all sentient beings.

Thank you to my family and friends whose endless love, support and belief provide constant inspiration and wonder.

A big hug and thanks to Sandy, my big sister, and Liza, my soul sister.

Thank you to my clients and students. Your love, light and grace remind me that we are a part of all we have met.

A big thank you to Dave, my cat companion, a sweet, nutty, healing being who keeps me on track.

While writing the guidebook for this card deck, my heart broke into pieces as I navigated the death of my mother; Amethyst, my cat companion of seventeen years; Lyra, the kitten; and my marriage. I am grateful to have been loved by these beautiful beings, and I hope I brought love, fun and grace into their lives.

CONTENTS

Introduction
Welcome, Illuminated One 11
The Language of Darkness 13
Your Shadow Name 15
Working with *The Secret Language of Darkness* 17
Using the Cards for Readings 19
Shadow Spreads 23
The Secret Language of Darkness and Light Spreads 26
The Shadow Mastery Classes 29

Card Meanings
1. Shadow Name 34
2. Golden Shadow 37
3. In the Sway of Influence 40
4. Reflection 44
5. Cycles and Patterns 48
6. Overthinking 51
7. Flexibility 55
8. Self-Awareness 59
9. Dark Night of the Soul 63
10. Spiritual Warrior 67
11. Desire 70
12. Secrets 74
13. Guilt 78
14. Resistance 82
15. Compassion 86
16. Forgiveness 89
17. Reimagine 92

18. Surrender 95
19. Endings 99
20. 2020 Vision 103
21. World Shadow 107
22. Worry 110
23. Triggers 114
24. Defence Mechanisms 118
25. Stress 123
26. Separation 127
27. Journey into Darkness 131
28. Conflict 136
29. The Bigger Picture 140
30. Nyctophilia 144
31. The Wounded Child 148
32. The Wounded Adult 152
33. Heart Love 156
34. Intimacy Shadow 160
35. Grief 164
36. Transcend 168
37. Anger 171
38. Dream Work 175
39. Projection 179
40. Judgement 183
41. Shadow Song 187
42. Integrity 190
43. Integration 194
44. Resilience 197
45. Fulfilment 201

ABOUT THE AUTHOR 205
ABOUT THE ARTIST 207

INTRODUCTION

Welcome, Illuminated One

I am so pleased and honoured you are here. This deck is sunshine radiating fresh insights into your awareness. It is a special torch shining into your darkest corners to integrate the abandoned and disowned and bring you to wholeness. These cards will lift anything that needs to be examined and healed out of the shadow. When you realise and acknowledge all perspectives, it is unlikely an event, situation or relationship will negatively trigger you. Instead, you will have access to the wisdom that will flow into sparks of "aha!" and understanding.

We create darkness as a coping mechanism for emotions and trauma we don't know how to process. It is not nasty, vile or demonic but a place to retreat or hide challenging aspects of our experience. Because we create it, we can also heal it!

Self-discovery is a beautiful, brave and liberating process. It expands perspective and allows us to experience synchronistic opportunities. All becomes possible when we empower our inner worlds and are open to new ideas. This is a founding concept of my oracular trinity with this deck, *The Secret Language of Light* and *The Secret Language of Manifestation*.

The Secret Language of Darkness reveals thoughts, ideas or beliefs that counter the nourishing possibilities available to you. These obstacles can make us feel tested or that we have done something wrong. Neither is true. When outdated beliefs are understood, cleared and released, we are free to embrace a path of promise and potential.

The card messages and shadow mastery classes are designed to pull back the veil and expose anything keeping you from your true loving self. It takes courage to face the repressed and unconscious aspects of our personalities. However, I know you are ready to liberate your mind, body and soul, that you are powerful, tenacious, and determined to live to your highest potential. How do I know this? Because you are here, reading this right now, poised and ready to open the door to the great mystery of you.

In harmony with all,
Denise

The Language of Darkness

This guide can consistently lead you to your authentic truths by illuminating and healing the unknown, the hidden and the denied. The language of darkness alerts us to imbalance through difficult emotions, thoughts, experiences, circumstances or situations. Until we know differently, we may react to these messages in ways that cloud their meaning. This can include denying, avoiding, repressing, suppressing, projecting, justifying or accepting that we can't escape a flawed fate.

When something feels terrible or amiss, it doesn't mean we have done anything wrong or are being punished or on the wrong path. It can remind us that we have split from the wisdom of the soul and may have fallen under the spell of another's truth. There are many truths on this planet — our job is to work with those we resonate with and let others believe theirs.

The darkness is a womb for incubating dreams and desires. It is a black velvety matrix, a field of infinite possibilities — a beautiful, loving steadfast space to return to and be held in safety and love. Here, we can release, heal and create something new from what we have already made. As we experience more, we constantly become more, and as we expand, the Universe expands alongside us. It is wonderful to have an in-built guidance system that alerts us when we conflict with soul wisdom and helps us adjust our sails.

Knowing Your Shadow

An inner repository of all the sensations and experiences you have disowned, your shadow is part of you, and it longs to be embraced and belong. Sometimes it can seem like a naughty child acting out to get your attention! Your shadow is trying to help, not hurt you. It is unbalanced energy, seeking balance. Harmony is a key that unlocks the door to your highest potential.

Soul Light Transmissions Wisdom from our Shadow

Your soul constantly communicates with you, sending forth information to lovingly illuminate your truth. Soul transmissions are subtle waves of energetic messages that are unique to you. This information is revealed in everyday situations to let you know where and when you hold yourself from your balanced centre. This type of communication may feel personal — and it is. But it is not hostile. It is your soul guiding you towards freedom.

By their very nature, the feelings of the shadow can be daunting. Your truth pushes against blocks to your authenticity, and they push back. To be free of the cycle of resistance, breathe into and beyond the discomfort and let all be as it is. Keep breathing through the process of allowing, as hurt dissipates and tension and tightness leave your body. When you let go of resistance, you become an active and conscious participant in your healing, where you may otherwise feel you are being dragged through the process. The choice is yours.

Your Shadow Name

Your shadow name personalises the darkness and makes it seem less scary. The mind finds it easier to communicate with a name rather than a concept. Your shadow name is a point of reference where you can meet your subconscious in all its forms. Using a name also makes it easier to recognise the feeling of your shadow, so you can put systems in place to understand and heal any aspect of it. The meditation in Card 1, *Shadow Name*, will help you discover your shadow name.

Denise's Shadow Name

The name of my shadow is *Korē* (aka Persephone). I was surprised when this name came to me. However, I honour her and aim to become the queen of my Underworld for healing and freedom.

Persephone is the goddess of the Underworld, springtime, flowers and vegetation. She is the daughter of Demeter, goddess of the harvest, and Zeus, king of the gods. Hades, the Underworld king, became captivated by Persephone, kidnapped her and made her his wife.

Demeter looked everywhere for her child to no avail. Her sadness caused her to neglect her duties. Crops died, and the land became lifeless. Zeus discovered what happened and confronted Hades about the abduction of his daughter. Persephone, however, had eaten several pomegranate seeds, which bound her to the Underworld. So, Zeus and Hades came to a compromise: Persephone would return to Demeter each spring, and at the end of summer, she would return to the Underworld to be with Hades.

Persephone did not readily accept her life and, feeling

imprisoned by Hades, fell into depression. However, she embraced her shadow over time and became Queen of the Underworld.

Here are some of the shadow behaviours the story of Korē has helped me understand and transform:

- Allowing my mother to emotionally manipulate me into going against my truth to please her.
- Dumbing myself down to make the men in my life feel more in charge and better about themselves and to make myself seem more attractive.
- Deliberately holding back from developing my career because I didn't think I was worthy of success, was scared of failing and thought I would be alone.
- Growing up too quickly and creating overly responsible and controlling behaviours as a child while simultaneously being fearful of maturity.

How Korē has helped me to step up:
- Even when life brings challenges, I can be and become the best version of myself.
- I now understand how adversity creates my passion for being happier.
- I accept that change is constant. I can adjust and adapt, just like the seasons.
- I have the tools and wisdom to work with any circumstance, whatever happens.
- I know it is up to me to live my mission and not rely on others for my identity or for love.

Working with *The Secret Language of Darkness*

Your shadow has inspired you to rendezvous with these cards to discover, heal and integrate pain, trauma or any other obstacles to your best life. Each time you work with this oracle, you enter a sacred gateway carved with the axiom 'Heal Thyself'. As you step through this threshold, you will liberate your knowledge and awareness of your shadow aspects. You have the strength and wisdom needed to look at your whole self, but when you feel unsure, remind yourself to go gently. Think of these cards as a personal spiritual assistant, helping you fine-tune your connection to the authentic you.

Each card has a message and a shadow mastery class. The message will tell you what is significant in your life now and how that may unfold. The shadow mastery class will delve deeper into the topic through meditation, inspired insights and journal work.

Managing Resistance

When deliberate actions build positive momentum, lasting change happens more organically. There will be days when your mind challenges your new approach. When this happens, you can choose to respond in one of the following ways:

- Breathe deeply and meditate.
- Have a rest day to adjust and adapt to your new perceptions. Don't give it another thought — just begin again tomorrow.
- If you want to carry on, remember that when you push against

resistance, it can push back even harder. Let it be there, let it have its opinion and say to that part of yourself, "I respect and honour your opinion; after all, it is a long-held belief that has become part of my everyday way of being. But just for today, I want to try something different."

You are at the beginning of a profound shift in your thinking. Be patient with yourself, as some beliefs are easier to let go of than others. It's okay to feel overwhelmed or to have off days. Be gentle with yourself and get in touch with a counsellor, therapist or trusted friend anytime you'd like support.

Using the Cards for Readings

The Welcome
This deck has found its way into your life because you are ready to feel, hear and see the messages within. Welcome your deck by holding it to your heart. Feel the energy flow from the cards into your heart, illuminating your creative, intuitive powers.

Preparing to Give a Reading
The calmer and more balanced you are when doing inner work, the clearer your answers will be. A receptive heart and mind will help you let go of issues, worries or problems for the duration of the reading. This meditative state will help you greet your shadow in a balanced, non-judgemental and loving way. Step outside judgement and assumption. Even if you have done this work many times before, give your shadow the ability to shine by imagining you are seeing it for the first time. Be present in the NOW. Allow everything to be as it is, uninfluenced by the past or the future.

The Intention
Before each reading, establish your intention with an invocation or meditation. This invites the presence of your angels, guides or light beings and connects you to the wisdom of your heart.

Sit quietly with your cards in your hands and close your eyes. Breathe gently and imagine the white light of the Universe flowing into the room, swirling all around you. Breathe in the light, knowing it is filled with unconditional love and healing. This illuminates a small golden light in your heart centre. This is your light of awareness, a guiding presence full of warmth and joy.

As you rest in the love and wisdom of your sacred light, gently open your eyes. You are now ready to start your reading.

The Question

If you don't have a question, you can leave the message up to the Universe, knowing that the information will always be for your highest growth with love.

If you have a question, phrase it so it requires more than a 'yes' or 'no' answer. Ask yourself what it is you want to know. For example, "Will I get this job" might become, "What are the opportunities and challenges of accepting this job?" The question of whether you and your beau will get married might be posed as, "How will my relationship with [name] progress over the next two years?" Be specific and use names and time frames where applicable. By changing the wording, you open the reading to more possibilities.

The Shuffle

Pick up your deck. If you have a question, hold it in your mind as you handle the cards. Shuffle or rearrange them in a way that is easy for you. You may like to cut the deck if this feels right. You can take the cards from the top or fan them out and choose from anywhere in the deck. The more you play with your cards, the sooner you will find the best way for you. Remember, there is no right or wrong way to do this.

Spreads

When we lay cards in a set pattern or order, it is called a spread. When using a spread, each card's message is considered in combination with the cards around it. This allows different pathways and perspectives to be introduced to the reading.

Jumping Cards

A jumping card is one that falls or 'jumps' out of the deck. Take note of jumping cards as they offer a magical insight into what you were feeling or understanding at the time they jumped.

Reversed Cards

When a card is dealt upside down, it can be read as reversed. Some readers attach importance to reversed cards, and some don't. There are no rules here. As always, do what feels best for you. In my experience, a reversed card may indicate delays and obstacles or that more information is to come. Remember, the language of darkness tells us where we are holding ourselves away from our desires and truths. So, what is perceived as an obstacle could be an angel in disguise.

The Future

Our lives are lived in the present, with the future unfolding one moment at a time. When reading future trends, allow the information and insight to illuminate all the options and possibilities before you. This will enable you to make empowered, informed decisions that will shape and influence future outcomes in the present. When the future arrives, it will be now.

Training Your Intuition

Each time you choose a card or lay out a spread, place the images face up. Look at the images one at a time, close your eyes and imagine yourself in each picture. What do you feel? What sensations, words or images come to you? Write down everything. Spend thirty seconds to a minute doing this, and then look up the card meaning in the guidebook.

Shadow Spreads

These spreads have been designed for this deck to offer clarity and healing in your readings. Please feel free to use your favourite spreads. You are welcome to incorporate wisdom from the Shadow Mastery Classes into your readings if you, or a client, want to delve a little deeper.

The Oracle of Your Shadow: Single-Card Spread

Shuffle the deck. Close your eyes if you like. Fan out the deck and choose one card with any hand. This card represents something extraordinary you need to recognise or learn to love about yourself.

```
┌─────────┐
│         │
│    1    │
│         │
└─────────┘
```

Close your eyes and breathe the image in and out. Allow yourself to relax in the knowledge you are opening to deep inner wisdom and love that has been in the shadows. After a while, you will move beyond the image into your inner world of creation.

When you feel ready, bring your focus back to the card image, breathe it in and out, open your eyes, and read the message.

Shadow Message: Two-Card Spread
This quick spread delivers a message from your shadow.

Card 1: Now — How the shadow turns up in your emotions or mood.
Card 2: Message — A way to balance your emotions or mood.

Shadow Vision: Four-Card Spread
Use this spread to gather insight into the predominating shadow energies affecting your life.

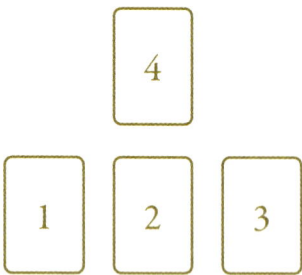

Card 1: Now — The part of your shadow being revealed today.
Card 2: Past — Something that is outdated but still keeps turning up in your life.
Card 3: Future — Something you need to change or embrace to live your dreams and desires.
Card 4: Sabotage — The obstacles you are placing on your path.

Shadow Healing: Four-Card Spread

Here is a small but powerful spread to reveal what you are currently energetically aware or unaware of.

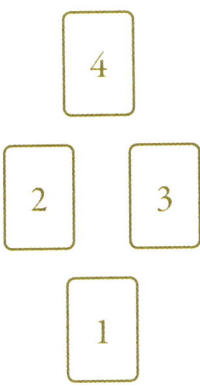

Card 1: Now — The most dominant shadow theme in your energy field. This card reveals what the majority of your thoughts are focused on.

Card 2: Love — The most dominant light theme in your energy field. This card shows what you are already clear on and good at. Focus on this to receive more of it.

Card 3: Fear — The illusion, belief or story clouding your perception. This card alerts you to fear so you can choose something different and let it fall away from lack of attention.

Card 4: Healing — What you can do to heal the illusion, belief or story; shows where deep healing is taking place.

THE SECRET LANGUAGE OF DARKNESS AND LIGHT SPREADS

You can use this deck on its own or in conjunction with its companion deck, *The Secret Language of Light*. The card numbers correspond to offer you a more profound understanding of your potential and its obstacles. For example, Card 9 in *The Secret Language of Light* is *Soul Journey*, and Card 9 in *The Secret Language of Darkness* is *Dark Night of the Soul*. Together, these cards tell the story of your soul journey and how outdated beliefs and ideas can be released. You can combine the cards or choose a card from one deck and then gain further information by selecting a card from the other. I've included two spreads here that use both decks.

LIGHT AND DARK MESSAGE: TWO-CARD SPREAD

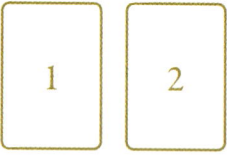

Card 1: Light message — Choose a card from *The Secret Language of Light*. This card reveals something your soul wants you to embrace.

Card 2: Dark message — Choose a card from *The Secret Language of Darkness*. This card reveals something that is preventing you from embracing your light.

Light and Dark Healing: Eight-Card Spread

This spread brings the two decks together to help you understand and heal your inner relationship with light and dark. It is okay to use this spread with one or more other oracle decks. Experimentation delivers additional information.

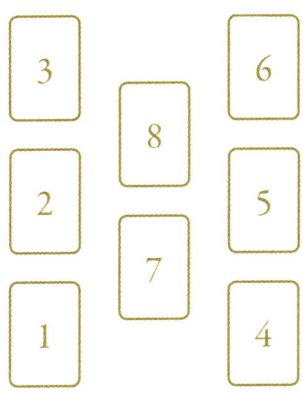

First, choose cards from *The Secret Language of Light*.

Card 1: Embrace — What your light wants you to recognise and integrate.

Card 2: Nurture — What your light wants you to accept and develop.

Card 3: Release — What your light wants you to detach from and clear.

Card 7: Merge — How your light intends to unite with your darkness.

Then, choose cards from *The Secret Language of Darkness*.

Card 4: Embrace — What your darkness wants you to recognise and integrate.

Card 5: Nurture — What your darkness wants you to accept and develop.

Card 6: Release — What your darkness wants you to detach from and clear.

Card 8: Symbiosis — How your darkness intends to cooperate and move forwards with your light.

THE SHADOW MASTERY CLASSES

The shadow mastery class included with each card will help you navigate the darkness and have direct contact and experience with the parts of you that have been or are sabotaging your dreams and desires.

When we choose to enter the unknown or shadow aspects of ourselves, it's important to understand that they are shrouded in the corners of our inner being and can jump out and knock us off-centre. They can make us feel unsafe and fearful because they trigger memories, stories or beliefs of a similar vibration. We will have come to conclusions about these triggers based on what we have been taught, the emotions we had at the initial experience or the need to fit in and be accepted.

Before you decide to enter your unknown, clarify your intention. Are you ready to face and feel your fears? Some fears can help us be rational. They alert us to something in our environment we need to avoid. So rather than talking about our fears over and over, let's explore them, understand them, resolve them, and be strengthened by them.

So, are you ready to walk into the dark?

Access your inner knowing and trust your gut and soul wisdom to feel your way through. If you feel uncomfortable, stop what you are doing, breathe deeply, bring your hands to the middle of your chest and centre yourself. If you are struggling or feel wobbly, let the process go for the time being and come back to it when you feel stronger.

Don't try and do this when you are feeling out of sorts. When your mood or vibration is down, you cannot trust how you perceive yourself or your situation. Everything will be seen through the filter of your low mood. In this state, you may struggle to see the answer or find your way out of the darkness, and you may spiral further into the shadow. If this is how you feel, be neutral for a while. You can also use the information in the previous section on managing resistance.

To use the deck for the shadow class, begin at Card 1 and work through the 45 cards, one after the other. Once you have finished all the cards, you can randomly choose a card when you feel you want to delve deeper and work with the information for self-inquiry. The information may be the same, but you are meeting it from a higher vibration and will experience expanded wisdom.

You can choose a card as often as you like, but I suggest you complete all the sections before moving on to another card so the information can be integrated into your daily life. Information never teaches. It remains a concept until it is experienced. Once experienced, you will begin to feel and understand it throughout your body and decide whether to adopt the material or let it go.

While you are coming to a decision or conclusion, I encourage you to do a reading using any of the spreads included to help clarify and consolidate your shadow and inner truth. You can add the information to your readings for expanded knowledge or a more profound healing experience.

The Three Sections of the Shadow Mastery Classes

Meditation

The meditation exercises are a way to connect to and understand the topic of the card more deeply. Meditation is a way to relax the body, quiet the mind and be fully present in the now. When you are relaxed and still, it becomes easier to tune in to your inner wisdom. Meditation is also a way to experience the images and words through your inner world of imagination.

The meditations are written in the present so you can experience the creative wisdom of your soul each time you listen to them. I suggest you record the meditations on your smartphone, tablet or computer with your own voice, then close your eyes while listening to the playback. As your voice is unique to you, it is another way the transmissions of your soul can flow and heal. You may also like to play some gentle music or burn some incense or aromatherapy oils.

Inspired Insights, Reflections and Actions
The reflections and actions consolidate and clarify the card's theme, sometimes adding actions that you can pursue. Sit with each statement or activity to discover what they mean to you. Think of yourself as a self-inquiry scientist.

Journal Work
You can ground your experiences through writing or drawing. When anchored, your experiences become a part of your everyday life, where you can choose what to keep and what to leave on the path.

Many beautiful journals are available for purchase, but you can also use your computer, other electronic devices or an exercise book. Allow your inspiration to choose. A journal is an invaluable record of your creative experiences and will serve as a reference for the future.

* * *

Self-discovery is a beautiful, brave and liberating process. It begins with an expanded perspective that allows us to experience synchronistic opportunities that enter our lives. All becomes possible as we focus and empower our inner worlds and are open to new ideas.

CARD MEANINGS

1. SHADOW NAME

Unlock the Mystery of Your Shadow

Liberate your shadow from darkness. Shine light upon them and say hello. Greeting your shadow begins a process that releases suffering and helps you feel free. Your shadow name personalises your darkness and gives you a way to explore and heal your shadow in a balanced and safe manner. When you shine light into the darkness, you release your fear of the unknown, anxiety dissipates, and you see what you thought were demons are angels in disguise. Ask for and be open to receiving the name of your shadow. It may arrive in a way you don't expect, but when it comes, you will know it is authentic by the way it feels. You are in the process of exploring and illuminating your inner world.

Shadow Mastery Class: Discover Your Shadow Name

Meditation

Place a hand on the card. Gently close your eyes. Sense your body and concentrate on your breathing. Follow your breath inward. Hold for five seconds and relax. Breathe out and release all tension. Focus on the middle of your chest.

In front of you, a golden staircase descends into the earth. Walk down the ten healing steps to a magical, amethyst crystal cave. Each step brings a sense of relaxation and ease. You are entering this mysterious space deliberately. There is no reason to be afraid. This undertaking is on your terms. Go as far as you want. Each time you enter this space, you will move a little further than before. Do what feels acceptable to you — there is no right or wrong way to do this. Honour this sacred interaction between you, your soul and your shadow.

The amethyst cave is the entrance to your shadow place. A single candle casts a subtle golden glow that reflects each facet of the amethyst that lines the cave. In this dimly lit space, your third eye activates your intuitive self, allowing you to feel your way through.

Find a place to sit in the cave. Inhale and, in your mind, introduce yourself and ask your shadow what you can call it. Your intention opens a door in the cave, and an invisible wave of empowerment flows into your third eye. Your shadow name moves on this wave — be open to receiving it. If you can't see, hear or feel a name, know it will come to you in the following days. In this space, old beliefs, limitations and stuck energies loosen and fall away. Bathe in the glory of empowerment for as long as you like — at least thirty seconds.

When you feel ready, close the door with your shadow name on it and leave the cave. Ascend the ten golden steps. Each step brings you closer to the physical world. At the top of the stairs, take two deep breaths and open your eyes.

Welcome back, brave, wise soul.

Inspired Insights, Reflections and Actions

Your shadow loves you. It has stored away all the things you thought would hurt or weren't ready to integrate into your experience. When you allow integration, all in your shadow becomes wisdom. Until that time, it unconsciously manages your perception and reactions. Open yourself to receiving the sounds your shadow is sending you. If necessary, ask for the communication to be louder or more precise. Ask your mind to be still as you do this. Trust all that comes to you. When you find a name or names, try them on to see how they feel. State out loud, "My shadow name is _____." It might feel scary and awkward at first but keep going. You will know when it is right for you when you feel a sense of relief, a rush of energy, a tingling, a revelation, a quiet recognition or a knowing.

Journal Work

For seven consecutive days, say the name or names you are trying out. Then write down at least two "aha!" moments this name or names invoke in you. This process helps you to see beyond your fears and appreciate the wisdom of your experiences.

2. GOLDEN SHADOW

Discover Deep Dreams and Desires

Beneath the shadow is the golden shadow. Desires from your golden shadow are bubbling upwards with renewed passion and drive. It contains dreams and desires you or another told you were not possible because of your gender, race, culture or societal expectations. You pushed them deep down because you didn't know how you could create them in your life. Your beliefs set limits on what you can create. Your job is to know—really know in your gut, heart and mind—that something is possible. Every dream and desire gains momentum when you believe it is possible. However, you may choose to keep that knowledge to yourself until you are sure. *The dismissive attitudes of others can make you doubt yourself and cause your dreams to retreat into the golden shadow.*

Shadow Mastery Class: Mine Your Gold

Meditation

Place a hand on the card. Gently close your eyes. Sense your body and concentrate on your breathing. Follow your breath inward. Hold for five seconds and relax. Breathe out and release all tension. Focus on the middle of your chest.

In front of you, a golden staircase descends into the earth. Walk down the ten healing steps to a magical, amethyst crystal cave. Each step takes you closer to your hidden talents, creativity and dreams. Step into the amethyst cave and greet your shadow. In front of you is an elevator with 'Golden Shadow' written in luminous gold on the doors. The doors open, and you enter. The doors slide shut, and as the elevator moves downward, you sense a lightness of being.

The elevator dings as it comes to a stop, and the doors open. You are greeted by shimmering light emanating from a treasure trove of ideas, potential, thought experiments, childhood dreams and fascinations. Walk among them and feel wonderment and relief as you reunite with your golden shadow. Let this energy permeate every part of you. Stay here for as long as you like — at least thirty seconds.

When you are ready, the doors to the elevator open. You step in, as does your golden shadow that wants to be integrated and actualised into your everyday life. The elevator whizzes upwards very fast. The doors open, and you step into the amethyst cave. As you ascend the golden staircase, vow that your dreams and desires will always be in the light. Even if you don't know how they will manifest, let them be with you. Ask yourself, "What actions can

I take to bring my inner gold into my everyday life?" The answers will drop into your mind in the following days.

Acknowledge your bravery for being your own hero. Thank your shadow for caring for your goldenness. At the top of the stairs, take two deep breaths and open your eyes.

Welcome back, wise gold soul.

Inspired Insights, Reflections and Actions
Your dreams are valid; don't allow another to tell you otherwise. Prioritising someone's dreams over your own can introduce doubt that pushes dreams into your golden shadow. If you want to do something, you will find a way, no matter how long it takes. If you don't, you will find an excuse. Take notice of who you admire. You possess the same potentials and qualities as those you admire. Appreciate, nurture and believe in those qualities in yourself.

Journal Work
Create a special place in your journal called 'My Gold'. Every time you have an idea, thought, desire or dream, write it in this place. No idea is too small or trivial; it is all a part of your creative process and needs to be honoured and celebrated. You can note your ideas on a scrap of paper or on an electronic device throughout the day, but I suggest transferring them into your journal after your daily meditation or before you go to bed. This physical practice embeds the energy of your ideas, like planting a seed.

3. IN THE SWAY OF INFLUENCE

Create with Your Authentic Self

As you go about your everyday life, your thoughts will be influenced by your authentic self, inner wisdom, friends, strangers, the media, society, cultural beliefs and more. When you are influenced by your inner wisdom, you are a cooperative part of the creation process. You will receive impulses from your authentic self that inspire you towards desired outcomes. When you act on these impulses, you will feel freer and more aligned with your nature. When an external influence is not conducive to your purpose or wellbeing, the creation process may feel a little off or wobbly. Should you be influenced onto a path that is not your own, it may lead to self-sabotage, disappointment or feeling like you are being tested. Should you feel this way, remember that nothing has gone wrong. Those feelings are a sign to shift your attention to your soul wisdom and seek its stabilising and freeing influence. Feel your way through!

Shadow Mastery Class: Sensing Your Influence

Meditation

Place a hand on the card. Gently close your eyes. Sense your body and concentrate on your breathing. Follow your breath inward. Hold for five seconds, breathe out and release all tension. Focus on the middle of your chest.

In front of you, a golden staircase descends into the earth. Walk down the ten healing steps, deepening your alignment with your inner wisdom as you descend. Enter the amethyst cave at the bottom of the staircase and greet your shadow. In front of you is a curtain of shimmering light. Part the curtain and walk into 'The Influence Room'. You are greeted by nebulous clouds of colour, warping and shifting, giving the impression of a hallucinogenic trip. You are safe here. Relax and witness your expanding awareness.

Among the colours, you notice four floating, coloured discs. The grey disc holds outside influences, the blue retains your truth, the pink mirrors your heart, and the golden disc is the keeper of wisdom. Each disc triggers different sensations to help you untangle your truth from outside influences. Breathe through this process and observe how you feel.

Step onto the grey disc and let the influences from the outside world flow to you one at a time. How do they feel? Do they help or hinder?

Now, step onto the blue disc and let your truth flow. How does it feel? Do you listen and trust it? Does it help or hinder?

Next, step onto the pink disc and open yourself to the love of your heart. Do you like how you feel? Listen to your instincts and feel them leading you to create more love in your world.

Finally, step onto the golden disc and allow all the information from the grey, blue and pink discs to merge and become wisdom. With wisdom, you can recall your stories without attachment. What stories do you tell, and how do they influence you? Some may inspire or infatuate, and some may scare or repel. Your reactions will clarify how your memories and what you tell yourself influence you.

As you continue to stand on the golden disc, allow your stories to drift in and out of your thoughts. Watch them come and go. When an uncomfortable story or memory floats forwards, stay detached. Leave it to merge back into the swirl of colour. When something feels right, let it inspire your passion. Allow the golden disc to surround you with golden light, healing all things that hold you away from your wisdom. Stay here for as long as you like — at least thirty seconds.

Your golden disc floats through the parted shimmering curtain of light. You step off into the amethyst cave. The disc floats back through the curtain as it draws shut. Take yourself to the golden staircase. As you ascend, notice that you feel more confident and clear.

Thank your shadow for giving you these fantastic choices. At the top of the stairs, take two deep breaths and open your eyes.

Welcome back, wise one. Practise connecting to inspiration daily, and it will become your influence.

Inspired Insights, Reflections and Actions

Even when you are focused elsewhere, it doesn't mean your inner self is. It is constantly gathering cooperative elements to create your desires. All you need to do is tune in.

Consider and try the following:

- Before making a decision, step back and consider all that might be influencing you: beliefs, ideas or expectations (yours or other people's), patterns, family, and culture or societal values.
- Change the pictures and words in your head. When you decide that the new story is possible, tell your mind what you want.

Journal Work

Write down or draw five internal influences and five external influences. This list is a part of your unique light language. It speaks to your feelings and emotions, sharing ways to focus and calibrate your soul wisdom. Say each influence out loud. Note whether it makes your heart shrink or sing. Heart-shrinking distances you from your wisdom. Heart-singing brings you closer to your soul wisdom. This process fosters self-awareness and helps you make unfettered decisions.

4. REFLECTION

Examine Thoughts and Feelings

Something has been occupying too much space in your mind and life. This card brings a clear message to create time to reflect on this matter so you can resolve and be free of it. While your focus keeps returning to this issue, it creates reflected information and evidence that validates your beliefs. For example, if you think about yellow cars, you will see them wherever you go. This is caused by a filtering system in the brain stem called the Reticular Activating System (RAS). It filters out uninteresting input so that you are not overwhelmed by irrelevant details and brings your attention to anything deemed important or that you are focused on. This filter also applies to your values and beliefs. The matter you've been preoccupied with has layers and facets that may be complicating or influencing your decisions. Contemplate and break the matter into its many parts. Then, do your best to step beyond its influence. Expand your beliefs and values so you can act in fresh ways and create novel experiences. For new adventures, ride the wave of self-reflection towards your dreams and desires.

Shadow Mastery Class: The Mirror Reflects Wisdom

Meditation

Place a hand on the card. Gently close your eyes. Sense your body and concentrate on your breathing. Follow your breath inward. Hold for five seconds and relax. Breathe out and release all tension. Focus on the middle of your chest.

In front of you, a golden staircase descends into the earth. As you walk down the ten healing steps to a magical, amethyst crystal cave, reflect on new ways to experience life.

Step into the amethyst cave and greet your shadow. In front of you is a holographic door. Step through the virtual door into a room containing three huge mirrors.

Look into the first mirror. A person, animal or thing you truly love appears in the reflection. Feel the love shining towards you. Open your heart to receive and send love back to what or who you love.

Gaze into the second mirror. A person, animal or thing you don't like is being reflected to you. Notice any uncomfortable feelings. This can be difficult but take a breath. And breathe into the uncomfortable feelings. Imagine any tender spots filled with your healing life force. Begin to heal and liberate any discomfort. You are doing so well.

Now, look into the third mirror. See your soul within the glass and feel unconditional love staring back at you. See the qualities of your soul: love, wisdom and bliss. Know they are within you. Allow new parts of your soul to be reflected. You are becoming more self-aware. Breathe in your potential. Stay here for as long as you like — at least thirty seconds.

Leave the mirror room through the holographic door of light and exit the amethyst cave. Walk to the golden staircase. As you ascend, reflections of your soul dance all around you. Each step gives you more meaningful choices and empowerment. Thank your shadow for reflecting all levels and dimensions of you. At the top of the stairs, take two deep breaths, open your eyes and realise you are more than you think you are.

Inspired Insights, Reflections and Actions

Consider the following:

- The most important relationship you have is with yourself. Every relationship you have, whether with a person, animal, situation, place, thing, thought or emotion, reflects this relationship. What do you like about yourself? Do you treat yourself the way you treat loved ones?
- Before you say anything in anger or judgement, stop, reflect and ask yourself, "Is this accurate, helpful and kind?"
- Research the Reticular Activating System (RAS) and mirror neurons.

Journal Work

Explore your relationship with the humans you first encountered — your parents or guardians. Whatever your experience with them, trust that they did the best they could, irrespective of their history. This exercise is not about forgiveness or blame; it is an unbiased reflection designed to expand your mind and consciousness with objective information. Write or draw three answers for each question so you can reflect on all sides in a balanced way.

- Who would I be if I had different parents/guardians?
- What kind of parents/guardians would I have preferred?
- What are the benefits of having the parents/guardians I have?
- What are the drawbacks of having the parents/guardians I have?
- How would I like to have benefitted from having the parents/guardians I preferred?
- What would be the disadvantages of having the parents/guardians I preferred?

5. CYCLES AND PATTERNS

Return to the Origin, Transform the Effect

You have become aware of repeating scenarios in your life. They may be with different people and in diverse situations, but it is undeniable — patterns have formed. Each time the cycle returns, it is amplified to gain your attention. Patterns contain familiar thoughts and beliefs that become entangled with your everyday way of living. Some patterns are helpful and supportive, but those that don't resonate with your soul truth can attract negative situations. It may feel that life is derailing you from your desired path. However, what you are experiencing is the result of beliefs that have outlived their usefulness. If you ignore a pattern, it can grow in intensity and repeat until, one day, you say, "Enough! I can't do, experience or be this anymore. It is time to change." When you interrupt the cycle, new paths are created and begin to emerge from your fresh perspective.

Shadow Mastery Class: Get Off the Merry-Go-Round

Meditation

Place a hand on the card. Gently close your eyes. Sense your body and concentrate on your breathing. Follow your breath inward. Hold for five seconds and relax. Breathe out and release all tension. Focus on the middle of your chest.

In front of you, a golden staircase descends into the earth. Relax as you walk down the ten healing steps to a magical, amethyst crystal cave. Each step brings forth deep insight into a pattern you unconsciously return to.

Step into the amethyst cave and greet your shadow. In front of you is a circular door with 'Breaking Patterns' written in red. The door opens, and you enter a spherical room. Look to your left. The story of your pattern begins to appear on the wall, depicted in comic form. Follow it around the room. As the story unfolds, it shows you aspects you were unaware of and reveals the underlying belief that drives the pattern.

Step into the centre of the room. Red healing light envelopes you. Insights will drop into your mind today or in the following days — the answers to why this pattern is so important and why you think it will make you safe or happy. Breathe in and be filled with red healing light. This will begin to break up the pattern. Stay here for as long as you like — at least thirty seconds.

Move over to the door, out of the circular room and into the amethyst cave. Walk to the golden staircase. As you ascend, you begin to feel lighter and empowered. Patterns and cycles can illuminate a part of you that is stored in your shadow. Thank your shadow for unfolding your patterns and spiralling them into your life as cycles. At the top of the stairs, take two deep breaths and open your eyes to freedom.

Inspired Insights, Reflections and Actions

Cycles recur due to our choices and behaviours. By responding to situations with the same approach, patterns are perpetuated. When those patterns are not helpful or rewarding, it's up to the individual to change them.

Patterns can help you understand so much about yourself, such as your motivations, coping mechanisms, and self-beliefs. You may feel your patterns are integrated with who you are. You may not know why you do the things you do. However, patterns begin with a single behaviour that becomes habitual and then ingrained in your everyday way of being. You can free yourself from these cycles in the same way — with one conscious response at a time.

Journal Work

Write about or draw a pattern you want to change. Add three statements about the behaviours that will help you to make that change. Then write about or draw how you will practise these behaviours in your daily life. Practise these behaviours for two weeks. Change occurs when you focus on the new way of being more than the old way of being.

6. OVERTHINKING

Redirect Your Focus to Change the Narrative

You have picked up a breadcrumb and mistaken it for a loaf of bread. The information you have is not the whole path. However, it will lead to more crumbs that will eventually form a clearer picture. Focusing on the breadcrumb and turning it over and over in your mind will elevate stress, diminish creativity and cloud judgement. Looking at an isolated detail can lead to the twisting of words, thoughts or narratives to invent desired outcomes. Our brains are hardwired to detect patterns that might satisfy the mind but are at odds with the heart. Merge your thoughts and feelings to create soul wisdom, also known as intuition. You will then recognise overthinking by the way you feel and can choose to redirect your focus and change the narrative. When you allow your mind to see beyond the crumbs to the nurturing whole, the energy will settle, and clear visions will appear.

Shadow Mastery Class: Your Mind is the Brain in Action

Meditation

Place a hand on the card. Gently close your eyes. Sense your body and concentrate on your breathing. Follow your breath inward. Hold for five seconds and relax. Breathe out and release all tension. Focus on the middle of your chest.

In front of you, a golden staircase descends into the earth. As you walk down the ten healing steps to a magical, amethyst crystal cave, feel the pathways in your mind as you reflect on new ways to experience life.

Step into the amethyst cave and greet your shadow. In front of you, a doorway is flashing as sparks run across it in all directions. Look closer and see the darting lights form pathways, like a chaotic map, across the door. Open the door and walk into the creative-sparks-of-your-thinking room.

Take a breath as you take in the magnificence of this creative space. Feel the tingle of electricity run through you like an aha or a light bulb moment. Thoughts are sparking in different colours all around you. Notice that some of the sparks are bigger and brighter than others. Direct the largest and brightest sparks into your heart and mind to inspire new neural pathways. The smaller and duller sparks are indifferent or not yet fully formed but may hold pertinent information for the future. Organise these thoughts by colour and move them to form a rainbow. As you interact with and shape your thoughts into this beautiful, sparkling image, notice the peaceful space, like a clear sky, that you have created around the rainbow. Connect with this space, breathe it in and feel it through your body. Know that this peaceful space is always present behind your thoughts and that you can connect with it whenever you wish.

Now, float deeper into that space until you come to a white crystal structure of a tree with branches dancing with stars. Feel each twinkle from the branches as a gentle sensation of joy, hope, love and possibility. You are experiencing the nature of your brain. This delicate creative dance is happening within you right now. Stay here for as long as you like — at least thirty seconds.

When you feel ready, thank the tree for its blessings and journey back to the rainbow. Connect again with the peaceful sky, then turn to find the sparkling doorway and re-enter the amethyst cave. Walk to the golden staircase, and as you ascend, feel the calm and peace of your uncluttered heart and mind. At the top of the stairs, take two deep breaths in and out, and say, "I am grateful for clear and loving thought, feeling and vision."

Inspired Insights, Reflections and Actions
Trust a decision and let it be. Constantly turning it over in your mind will introduce doubt. Soon enough, you will see the results and can decide on your next steps. As new pathways form, old ones naturally weaken and fall away. Eventually, through repetition, your new pathways will run on autopilot. You may benefit from researching Socratic thinking, rational thinking or Byron Katie's work.

Journal Work
Write or draw whatever comes into your mind. Scribble words or pictures. As you do this, you may feel agitated, frustrated, or muddled. Any feelings that arise are okay. Acknowledge them and allow them to spill onto the page with any pain or hurt. Your page

(or pages) may look messy or chaotic. There is no need to give meaning to what you place on the paper. This exercise is an outlet for excess energy caused by overthinking to flow away from you. Spend five to ten minutes in this process. Imagine all that clouds your wisdom is dismantling and vanishing.

7. FLEXIBILITY

The Ability to Adjust and Adapt

You may feel stuck and reluctant to move forwards if you haven't explored all the avenues and solutions available to you. Perhaps you feel unable to look beyond the problem, or your mind is locked in a pattern of fear or hopelessness. Either way, your beautiful loyalty is so devoted to a specific outcome with a person or situation that you can't see another way forward. Be loyal to your soul truth. Flex your empowerment muscles. Return to your centre—a neutral, calm place—to free your vision so other ways can come into focus. The yīnyáng symbol is a reminder that life is filled with lights and darks — there is light within the darkness and dark with the light. However, your filters, beliefs and ideas control your experience. Your mind and ego use them to keep you safe, like an overprotective carer might limit the fullness of life to shield a child from pain. When you explore and experience new ways, you will come to know how much you are truly capable of.

Shadow Mastery Class: Go with the Flow

Meditation

Place a hand on the card. Gently close your eyes. Sense your body and concentrate on your breathing. Follow your breath inward. Hold for five seconds and relax. Breathe out and release all tension. Focus on the middle of your chest.

In front of you, a golden staircase descends into the earth. Walk down the ten healing steps to a magical, amethyst crystal cave. As you do so, feel your mind and body soften. Know that nothing has gone wrong, and feel safe to see, experience and approach all that is before you, your past, present and future, in different ways. Step into the amethyst cave and greet your shadow. In front of you is a small round door with 'Mind Your Head' written on it. The door opens, and you find you can only enter it by crouching. It is tight, but you manage to shimmy through the door.

You are standing on the bank of a fast-flowing river. A giant yīnyáng symbol hangs in the sky, like a sun radiating all options, good and bad, the good in the bad and the bad in the good. The river represents the flow of your life as it moves and changes. You can choose to stay on the bank. However, as you are here, you can also choose to make the leap and jump in. It will be worth it to join and co-create with life. It doesn't matter where or when you enter the river of life. The difference comes in deciding to leap in to become a more active participant in your life, ready to work with the currents.

When you are ready to make that leap, say, "I am what I am. I am my truth. I am who I am, and what I seek is seeking me."

Take a deep breath and dive. Relax and allow yourself to be swept along. You may be tossed and tumbled in the fast-moving currents, but you are safe. Keep breathing, and as you refuse to cling to the old, the river, still moving fast, embraces you with a floating softness. Drift upon your river of life, allowing images, feelings and symbols to come to you. Flow here for as long as you like — at least thirty seconds.

The river winds and weaves until it returns you to the small round door. You gently float into the amethyst cave. Notice the door is now called 'Unguard Your Heart'. Walk to the golden staircase. As you ascend, feel your mind and heart reconciling to the possibilities of life. You are united and serene, fully accepting yourself and others. Thank your shadow for helping you flow with reality, even when you didn't want to. At the top of the stairs, take two deep breaths in and out, open your eyes and go with the flow.

Inspired Insights, Reflections and Actions

Approach a situation like a tree in the wind, ready to bend and bounce back tall and true. With this flexibility and knowing you cannot break, you will want to explore new directions. A flexible mind adapts to changing circumstances. Even when things don't work out precisely as you desire, you will see opportunities in new situations. Find and focus on joy in your environment. When you can't find happiness, coast along in neutral until something triggers joy.

Research fixed and growth mindsets. A fixed mindset assumes intelligence and talents are relatively static and can't be improved. A growth mindset understands that intelligence and skills can be developed and enhanced. You are constantly learning, growing in yourself and finding wonderful ways to respond to your world.

Journal Work

To refresh your experience of life, go into the world with curious eyes. The Buddhists call this 'beginner's mind'. To engage with this approach, try something for the first time, begin something anew or do the same old thing in a completely new way. Look around you and gaze at an object. Allow the name of the thing to fall away. If you didn't know the object's name or what it is used for, how would you explain the object? Look at its shape, form, colour and texture without judgement or assumptions. When you do this long enough, the object will become strange and unfamiliar, like when you say a word over and over until it loses its meaning. You will then experience a curious mind that asks, "What is that?" Curiosity opens the beginner's mind. Write or draw about what you just experienced.

8. SELF-AWARENESS

Observe from a Balanced Perspective

This card talks of the control the external world can have on our internal reality. Both unpleasant and pleasant experiences can influence, even direct and bind our thoughts. Unpleasantness can lead to anxiety or depression. Pleasure can lead to being reliant on something outside of yourself just to feel okay. While there is nothing inherently wrong with either scenario, when you look to the external world for validation, confidence or material worth, or to feel in control, liked or loved, you are relying on conditions being a certain way. It is time to take back control of your thoughts and focus attention on your unconditional inner world. The heart is your soul's perspective and the key to self-awareness. Turn inwards and become an unbiased witness to thoughts and emotional reactions. Align your vision with the way your authentic higher self and soul see. When you expand your awareness, you can easily become a conscious observer and make empowered choices.

Shadow Mastery Class: Know Thyself

Meditation

Place a hand on the card. Gently close your eyes. Sense your body and concentrate on your breathing. Follow your breath inward. Hold for five seconds and relax. Breathe out and release all tension. Focus on the middle of your chest.

In front of you, a golden staircase descends into the earth. Walk down the ten healing steps to a magical, amethyst crystal cave. Each step drops you into a more expansive awareness, mentally, physically and spiritually. Step into the amethyst cave and greet your shadow.

In front of you is a glass door etched with 'Watch Your Thoughts'. As you open the door and enter the room, you see it is filled with golden rays that evoke excitement.

The walls and ceiling slowly fade away to reveal the night sky. You feel safe as magic fills the air. Beams of starlight that shimmer and glow with stardust fall around you. Breathe in your golden light of wisdom. Let it fill your whole body with gentle warmth. You feel yourself lifting and floating towards the stars.

Among the stars, you meet a light being who introduces themself as your soul awareness. The light being gently guides you to a golden star that you understand to be your soul star chakra. A comfortable-looking couch made of clear quartz crystal sits at the centre. You sit on the couch together — you and your soul awareness. From this vantage point above your shadow room, your physical self appears as a bright point of light. Your whole life is visible from the past to the present and maybe a little of the future. You begin to understand why you have been so focused on external validation.

You see that past, present, and future events are connected to your values and beliefs. You realise that you are a co-creator of your circumstance. Thus, you could deliberately create your dreams and desires by directing your thoughts and emotions. You are willing to transform.

Gaze upon your physical self with great tenderness and send rays of awareness to any area of your life or body that needs balance. Keep sending healing light until you feel all is harmonious. Stay here for as long as you like — at least thirty seconds.

Float downward, back into the room and towards the glass door. As you move through the door into the amethyst cave, notice the etching has changed to 'Self-Realised'. Walk to the golden staircase. As you ascend, you realise you have just experienced your true nature. Thank your shadow for holding your self-awareness and realisation until you were ready to step into them. At the top of the stairs, take two deep breaths and open your eyes to a new world.

Inspired Insights, Reflections and Actions

When you don't tend to your energy, someone or something else will. You may become susceptible to advertising, crowd-thinking and domineering people — who may be well-meaning. When you seek answers in your mind, you search your archives and files from the past. You are absent from the present and unable to access self-awareness. If you feel angry or overwhelmed, step back and ask yourself, "What emotion will be more helpful right now? How can I connect to it?"

Journal Work

List these headings in your journal: health and fitness, intellect, emotions, spirituality, relationships and love, parenting yourself and others, social life, finance, career, family and friends. Jot down some words that describe what each area means to you. Then write down or draw the activities you do to support each area. Doing something to nurture these areas daily will help resolve any conflict between awareness and non-awareness.

9. DARK NIGHT OF THE SOUL

Ego Patterns Soften, and Soul Wisdom Emerges

You may be struggling to make sense of something that has happened or is happening now. As a consequence, you may be questioning your beliefs or the meaning your life had before. Our beliefs, purpose and perspectives provide safety. Challenging them takes bravery, and doing so can, for a short time, create a void within us. This 'dark night of the soul' can feel crushing, but on the other side, when the dawn comes, you will realise it is liberating. Think of Pandora opening her box and releasing pain and suffering. Once life's miseries had been let out, one thing remained in the box: hope. As you journey through your dark night, courageously questioning your purpose, your beliefs and who you are, you are freeing pain and disharmony from your inner world. Beneath it, you will find hope and peace. Should you feel like you are stumbling in the dark, know you are healing, growing and coming closer to hope. Keep going. Know that darkness and suffering are not the only pathways to peace. As you move to happier times, you will bring with you the power and strength to draw from the spring of your newfound harmony.

Shadow Mastery Class: Keep Your Eyes on the Hope Ahead

Meditation

Place a hand on the card. Gently close your eyes. Sense your body and concentrate on your breathing. Follow your breath inward. Hold for five seconds and relax. Breathe out and release all tension. Focus on the middle of your chest.

In front of you, a golden staircase descends into the earth. Relax as you walk down the ten healing steps to a magical, amethyst crystal cave. With each step, you feel yourself being drawn deeper into the silent space within — into your inner world.

Step into the amethyst cave and greet your shadow. In front of you is a door with 'Dark Night of the Soul' written on it. The door opens, and you enter a beautiful night landscape lit gently by a waning crescent moon. Due to the dim light, your steps are unsure and tentative at first. Soon you attune your senses to perceive a path — you are 'seeing' with your inner eye and feeling more confident. The path spirals downwards into your beautiful depths. As you follow the path, you notice the air is crisp and filled with the aroma of sage. You feel comfortable with the darkness and trust your inner senses to guide you through the unseen. You feel safe and protected and bless the darkness.

A bright light begins to shine from deep within you. This illumination is your inner day star, your sun, an inner source of light and warmth that is always accessible. A pleasant tingling sensation accompanies the glow that radiates from your body. Rays of healing spread through you as a gentle warmth. You are as comfortable with the dark night as with the daylight. Bless the appearance of the light as you blessed the darkness that preceded it. Let this energy permeate every part of you. Stay here for as long as you like — at least thirty seconds.

Begin to walk back along the spiral path. Now it is illuminated and bright, and answers reveal themselves as you move upward. Walk back through the door into the amethyst cave. The door's name has changed to 'Day Light of the Soul'.

Walk to the golden staircase. As you ascend, you understand that darkness leads to your light and potential. When you feel broken, light shines through the cracks to reveal once-hidden paths to your desires.

Acknowledge your courage in this transformational process, and thank your shadow for showing you the way when you thought you couldn't see it. At the top of the stairs, take two deep breaths and open your eyes. Welcome the light of your life.

Inspired Insights, Reflections and Actions

The dark night of the soul is a spiritual crisis that leads to illumination, as described by the Spanish monk Saint John of the Cross. Carl Jung expanded on this principle to include a psychological as well as a spiritual perspective. The dark night of the soul comes as an opportunity for change. It can be prompted by a crisis, but sometimes the exact reason is unclear. If you are going through a dark night, accept that the light will return and ride the wave. Pushing against it will not hurry the sunrise. Breathe, go into yourself and search for, wait for, your awakening truth. Moving your body can provide comfort and clarity during a dark night of the soul, as it allows stagnant thoughts and energy to shift and flow into the ground. Take your shoes off and walk or dance around the house. When you feel you can, go outside and walk on the grass. You may also like to try some yoga — research and try the series of yoga poses called 'Salute to the Sun'.

Journal Work

Write or draw about three times you thought you would never get through. Reflect on what these experiences have in common. Realise that you are much stronger than you ever thought.

10. SPIRITUAL WARRIOR

Discover and Honour Your Inner Courage

An uncomfortable feeling has been keeping you company. You may worry that it will become a constant companion, one that is unsupportive or limiting. Your first impulse may be to argue with this feeling or to push it away. Instead, be a spiritual warrior — face and embrace the discomfort without judgement. From this neutral place, the unpleasant feeling can communicate why it has arisen and what it wants. Your inner spiritual warrior is activated by courageous vulnerability. They are confident and have unwavering self-belief. They bring the mind and heart together where sacred truth can be accessed. The spiritual warrior will seek and act without any assurance. Whether a path leads to treasures or a dead end is not their concern. They undertake new activities, emotions and change without fear or resistance and speak up without blame or judgement. The spiritual warrior can move mountains, shift paradigms and address uncomfortable feelings before they become bigger issues. In doing so, they inspire others to discover their inner strength.

SHADOW MASTERY CLASS:
HONOUR YOUR TRUTH BY FACING AND EMBRACING FEAR

Meditation

Place a hand on the card. Gently close your eyes. Sense your body. Breathe deeply. Draw your attention inwards and relax. As you breathe out, release tension and focus on the middle of your chest.

See a golden staircase descending in front of you. Relax as you walk down the ten healing steps to a magical, amethyst crystal cave. With each step, you feel an inner strength rising from your feet to the top of your head. Step into the amethyst cave and greet your shadow.

In front of you is a spinning galaxy. As you step into it, misty and magical light swirls around you, lifting you onto Bifröst, the fiery rainbow bridge of Norse legend. Notice a wolf sitting next to you. This is your animal totem, a companion for your journey, here to invoke your instincts, personal power and self-control.

Take a step onto the bridge. Even though it is made of fire and light, it is safe and firm. Walk slowly and mindfully, enjoying every step. You are a pioneer, moving into unchartered territory, forging a path into a new way of being. This bridge spans your fears and limitations. Begin to feel them slipping away as you cross the bridge.

You reach the other side and are greeted by your spiritual

warrior. You embrace heartily. Allow your warrior to enter your heart and communicate their wisdom as you play with your wolf. Be who you are, for you have something unique and wonderful to share with the world. Stay here for as long as you like — at least thirty seconds.

On the way back over the bridge, feel yourself emitting newfound strength and freedom. Your fears are far below you now and do not concern you. Bask in and remember this inspirational feeling whenever you need to. Step off the bridge and through the spinning galaxy into the amethyst cave and say goodbye to your wolf.

Walk to the golden staircase. As you ascend, feel a quiet golden strength rising in you. Thank your shadow for guarding your spiritual warrior until you were ready to discover and step into their power. You have become more of you. At the top of the stairs, take two deep breaths and open your eyes to new confidence and unwavering self-belief.

Inspired Insights, Reflections and Actions
Try the following exercises:
- Consider going on a spiritual retreat to uncover personal truths and spiritual clarity and meet like-minded people.
- Research different spiritual warrior traditions, such as Shamanic, Toltec, Zen or Taoist.
- Research plant and herbal medicine.

Journal Work
Write down or draw three of your superpowers. These are qualities that others enjoy about you or things you love to do. Within these strengths, you can find and connect with your spiritual warrior.

11. DESIRE

Realising New Pathways of Becoming

You desire something new or different in your life. Your longing triggers a need for instant gratification. You believe that life will be better when you attain what you long for, but ask yourself, "Why do I desire this thing? Is it to fill a void or create bliss?" Are you ready for the changes this desire will bring? Your soul knows the purpose of life is experience. Life is about forging pathways, not the outcome. When you arrive at the manifested experience, new desires will arise. Wanting more … yearning for fresh horizons, learnings, connections, and experience … is the nature of creating. Allow this concept to sink into your mind and body and activate a deeper understanding of desire. Fulfilment comes from the journey. Be patient. Pick the fruit only when it is ripe.

Shadow Mastery Class: Create Pathways to Your Desires

Meditation

Place a hand on the card. Gently close your eyes. Sense your body. Breathe deeply. Draw your attention inwards and relax. As you breathe out, release tension and focus on the middle of your chest.

In front of you, a golden staircase descends into the earth. Relax as you walk down the ten healing steps to a magical, amethyst crystal cave. With each step, you feel excitement stirring deep within. The inception of new desires rises into your awareness. Step into the amethyst cave and greet your shadow.

In front of you is a small orange orb named 'Desire'. The orb grows in size until it is big enough for you to step inside it. When you do, you are transported with a whoosh into a swirling vortex of orange, red and yellow. You are safe. Allow yourself to be present in the source of your desire. You are unique. No one has ever experienced or seen life as you have and never will. Your desires, and the paths you take towards them, are also unique. They are a way for your soul and the Universe to experience and expand. Each desire, no matter what it is, produces growth. Nothing is off-limits. You are worthy and able to grow through each yearning that arises within you.

Now, focus on the feeling of your desires. See your desires as tiny points of light emerging from the colourful swirling vortex. A combination of passion, euphoria and delight fills your senses as your seeds of desire expand into countless spheres of light that float around you.

Reach out and touch one of your spheres. Begin to experience your desire in all its forms. See how it can be part of your life. As you do this, a doorway for inspired actions and solutions unlocks. In the following days and weeks, they will drop into your mind and heart. Engage with as many of the spheres as you wish. Stay in this sacred space for as long as you want — at least thirty seconds.

Move through the swirling vortex to the orange orb, and when you feel ready, step back into the amethyst cave. Walk to the golden staircase. As you ascend, feel your desires moving into your physical life, becoming palpable. Thank your shadow for nurturing and retaining your desires. It now hands the full creative responsibility back to you because you are ready. At the top of the stairs, take two deep breaths. Open your eyes and become your desires.

Inspired Insights, Reflections and Actions
Try the following exercises:

- Create a folder called 'Desire Box' on your electronic device. When a desire comes to you, add it to your folder. Every three months, go through it and discard what has manifested or what you no longer desire. You are decluttering your thoughts and clarifying what you truly want.
- Imagine your desires floating around you, waiting to drop into your awareness. Your focused energy will activate the pathway of manifestation.
- Imagine that all you desire, desires you! Are you ready for it?

Journal Work
Divide a page in your journal into three columns. In the first column, write or draw about three desires. (I found three to be a good number to work with — you can add as many as you like.) In

the second, write or draw what experiences inspired these desires. In the last column, write or draw how you will feel when these desires manifest in your life.

12. SECRETS

A Relentless Push to Freedom

What are you hiding from yourself or the world? Secrets eat away at your energy and limit full access to your soul's wisdom. We all have desires that we make secret or shameful due to external influences from culture, family or peer groups. But when we push our needs, wants or instincts down, they find ways to move through our resistance and can surface in unpredictable ways. Repressed truth often creates denial, deception or defiance. You may judge the very thing you are trying to conceal. There are instances where secrets or lies can help. However, in most cases, it is best to find a way to reconcile inner conflict before it hurts your self-esteem. Your soul will never judge you. Whether your experiences are good or bad, you still grow and expand with the world and the Universe. Past experiences created this present moment and have given you a choice and opportunities for growth and self-awareness. You have nothing to be ashamed of. Bring your hidden drives into the light, and they will teach you who you are.

SHADOW MASTERY CLASS: HEAL THE NEED TO KEEP SECRETS

Meditation

Place a hand on the card. Gently close your eyes. Sense your body and concentrate on your breathing. Follow your breath inward. Hold for five seconds and relax. Breathe out and release all tension. Then focus on the middle of your chest.

In front of you, a golden staircase descends into the earth. Walk down the ten healing steps to a magical, amethyst crystal cave. Each step reveals a hurt in your body caused by the secrets you hold. Step into the amethyst cave and greet your shadow.

When you look around, you see the amethyst above and to your sides. In front of you, the floor extends into the shadowy depths of the cave. You feel an impulse to walk deeper into the cave. Seemingly out of nowhere, a hidden door flings open. You walk through the door into a room filled with golden searchlights, looking for secrets. Your soul wants to shine a healing light upon them. Take a breath and be still. Allow your soul to bring your secrets to light so that wisdom, understanding and self-awareness can blossom. Observe your secrets with mindfulness. In the golden light, there is no judgement, shame, guilt or doubt, and each enlightened secret holds understanding and healing.

There are some secrets that you are ready to release. Do that now. Recognise how much energy it takes to compartmentalise and store the secrets you are not ready to share or let fall away. See how the walls of this room, which seemed strong, have cracks forming. Your secrets will not stay here — and this is not where they belong. It is time to begin the process of coming to peace with them. Collect the secrets, scooping them up in your arms. It is time to hand them over.

A beautiful, shimmering light being materialises in the room. This is your holder-of-secrets angel who carries a basket filled with healing golden light. You feel so loved as your eyes meet theirs. Place the secrets you are not ready to tell into the basket. Your angel will hold them without judgement. A sense of relief flows over you. When you are prepared to share them, your angel will hand them back to you. Your angel has a message for you: listen with an open heart. Stay here for as long as you like — at least thirty seconds.

You feel so light as you float back into the cave from the secret room. Walk to the golden staircase. As you ascend, aim to live in a way that means you don't need to keep secrets. Thank your shadow for holding your secrets. At the top of the stairs, take two deep breaths and open your eyes to freedom.

Inspired Insights, Reflections and Actions

The bigger the secret, the bigger the burden and the harder it is on your body. Not all secrets are bad, but living with the secret can cause stress and make us feel inauthentic. See the connection between your body and your mind and acknowledge any hurt or heaviness the secret may be causing your physical self. Tell your secret to an animal or a tree to release some of its burden.

Journal Work

Write down or draw secrets that are ready to be released. The act of letting them flow from your mind onto paper will continue the healing process begun in your meditation. You can then decide what you will do with the information. If you are not ready to share, soak or carefully burn the paper until it disintegrates. Allow this process to settle for a few days, then do it again. I suggest you do this once a month. Sometimes it takes time for secrets to rise into your awareness. Go easy.

13. GUILT

A Past Stronghold is No Longer True for You

The repercussions of a past action or creation are causing waves in the present. Look back and consider why you made the decisions you did. Others may say you should have known better, and perhaps you agree. Be open and truthful about your circumstance and intentions at that time. Did you lack the confidence to follow your judgement? Were you acting out of kindness, spite, hope, despair or something else? Only you know what your motivations were. If something truly needs to be forgiven, take responsibility, forgive your actions, and vow to do better. It's time to step forwards with a fresh heart.

Shadow Mastery Class: Dissolving the Grip of Guilt

Meditation

Place a hand on the card. Gently close your eyes. Sense your body and concentrate on your breathing. Follow your breath inward. Hold for five seconds and relax. Breathe out and release all tension. Focus on the middle of your chest.

In front of you, a golden staircase descends into the earth. Walk down the ten healing steps to a magical, amethyst crystal cave. Each step reveals a truth about guilt. While remorse leads to heart-honouring change, prolonged guilt is about self-judgement. It reinforces your mind's idea that you are flawed. Arrive at the last step, excited to confront your guilt.

Step into the amethyst cave and greet your shadow. In front of you is a heavy, antique wooden door with 'Guilt Trips' carved into it. Drag the door open and enter the room.

You are confronted with a pile of rocks. Each rock represents the guilt or regrets you feel over an action, thought or outcome. Climb and explore the rocks. You allowed this pile to grow. It has become an obstacle that causes resistance and procrastination and opens you to manipulation. But no more! It's now time to transform the heaviness of this guilt into remorse, grace and wisdom. Stand on top of your pile and ask for integration and healing.

A healing cloud with a silver lining floats into the room and begins to rain liquid light upon you. This unique light shower cleanses and calms you while gently dissolving your guilt.

As the pile shrinks into nothingness, say to yourself:

I trust my inner guidance. I know my truth. I integrate the lessons of the past and grow stronger in heart, mind and intention. My words and actions honour my core values. I am gentle with myself and others.

Let the shower of light flood your body with love until it fills every cell within you. Every cell born from this moment will be in complete balance. Stay here for as long as you like — at least thirty seconds.

You are liberated from guilt. It is time to leave the room. Know you can return at any time to release guilt if your pile begins to grow again. The door is now light enough to close with one finger. Close it now, step into the amethyst cave, and walk to the golden staircase. As you ascend, feel a renewed certainty and confidence in your truth and wisdom. Thank your shadow for holding your guilt until you were ready to dissolve it. At the top of the stairs, take two deep breaths, open your eyes and smile.

Inspired Insights, Reflections and Actions

While guilt can be a healthy message that you have behaved in a way that is not aligned with your values, prolonged guilt is a corruptive emotion. It is difficult to feel and address because it is an ego wound that sits in self-judgement. Our souls know we make mistakes and, where necessary, allows us the space for remorse through which we can assess our intentions and actions with clarity, honesty and a sincere desire to grow. Remember this should someone try to use guilt to manipulate you. Set healthy boundaries by affirming to yourself and others that acting out of guilt will create resentment.

Journal Work

Write or draw a list of no more than three mistakes you made as you grew up. These can be what you perceive as errors of thought or action. How were these mistakes handled? Were they forgiven, judged or punished? Who did the forgiving, judging and punishing? Do you still judge yourself by these standards? Ask yourself whether those standards reflect your true values.

14. RESISTANCE

Obstacles to Your Flow

You have done the work, read the books and even have sophisticated explanations for all that has and may happen to you. However, you are yet to fully integrate the great work you have done. There is more to your journey as you bring your insights from your head into your whole self. You are justifying beliefs, thoughts, actions or feelings that hold your deeper healing and desires at arm's length. It's time to hold them up to the light of the present and see beyond them. Open your heart and mind to who and where you are today. Dive into your truth, empowerment and compassion. Resisting your reality is denying your growth and potential. Step out of stasis and bring your attention to all you want in the here and now. Your mind and energy field can then reverberate with your soul's plans and possibilities. You may then see that life is not a test of your worthiness but something worth embracing. Seize it fully, without delay.

Shadow Mastery Class: Radically Accepting the Now

Meditation

Place a hand on the card. Gently close your eyes. Sense your body and concentrate on your breathing. Follow your breath inward. Hold for five seconds and relax. Breathe out and release all tension. Focus on the middle of your chest.

In front of you, a golden staircase descends into the earth. As you walk down the ten healing steps to a magical, amethyst crystal cave, your body relaxes, your mind becomes quiet and loving, supportive energy moves around you.

Step into the amethyst cave and greet your shadow. In front of you, a door labelled 'Radical Acceptance' is ajar. You peek inside and see a beautiful place in nature. This is your unique space where you feel completely at ease, immersed in the peace and glory of the natural world. The door swings open quickly, and you float through.

Take a breath and notice how the pristine air feels as it enters and leaves your body. Feel how good it feels to breathe. When you were born, your first action was to inhale and receive the breath of life. Your second was to exhale, giving breath back to the world in a new form. How fully are you receiving and giving? One does not occur without the other. Take a moment to notice whether your breathing feels constricted, sticky or uneven. Keep breathing until it feels even and deep.

Close your eyes and scan outwards with your senses. You will feel drawn to a location. Move towards it and scan again to find your power spot. Sit or lie down upon the earth. Gently notice what's present here with you — the sensations arising in your body and any movement of emotions or thoughts. Welcome it all. Allow it all to be here. Don't try to change it. Don't push it away or pull it towards you. Just let it all be the way it is. You are safe.

If any discomfort arises, respond with compassion. Embrace this pain as you would comfort a loved one or an animal or child. Love this part of you until balance and harmony fill your senses. Remain still and spacious in your awareness of all. Feel how wonderful it is to be at peace with yourself and all things. Stay here for as long as you like — at least thirty seconds.

Gently arise from your spot in nature and move through the door of radical acceptance into the amethyst cave. Walk to the golden staircase. As you ascend, notice how clear and precise your mind is. Inspiring ideas will come to you now or in the days and weeks to come as resistance falls further away. Thank your shadow for the internal opposition that reveals where you are ready to grow. At the top of the stairs, take two deep breaths in and out. Open your balanced, accepting eyes and welcome your new outlook.

Inspired Insights, Reflections and Actions
Try the following exercises:

- Research 'spiritual bypassing'. This phrase was coined in the 1980s by psychologist John Welwood. He observed the tendency to use spiritual practices and ideas to avoid facing unresolved emotional issues and psychological wounds.

- Pay attention to any resistance in your body. These feelings may reveal where you most need to embrace your emotions and shift your perception.
- Research 'cognitive dissonance'. This term refers to internal conflict that arises when beliefs, feelings, values, behaviours or observations don't align. Examples might be wanting to do well on an exam but choosing not to study for it or choosing to ignore a new piece of information because it challenges an existing view.

Journal Work

Write or draw about a time you felt resistance to something. It could have been a person, an idea or a change. Write or draw about how you knew you were resisting and where you felt it in your body.

15. COMPASSION

Co-creating Space for Passionate Inclusion

Your heart is expanding into a fuller acceptance of yourself and others, thus broadening your experience of emotion and feeling. Your capacities for kindness, charity, empathy and sympathy are increasing. This will raise your awareness of any prejudicial patterns. Should you find yourself drifting into any of those past patterns, confront them with gentle compassion. Rather than turning away, move towards your response with curiosity, kindness and love. Practise compassion towards yourself by acknowledging your learned reactions and how you are now creating habits of thought that are aligned with your expanded consciousness. To be compassionate is to co-create with care, kindness and passion. Observe those around you and how they are feeling. Return to your compassionate centre as needed. It is a calm and steady home from which you can accept yourself and others without judgement, honour your experiences and welcome lasting healing.

Shadow Mastery Class: Cultivating Kindness

Meditation

Place a hand on the card. Gently close your eyes. Sense your body and concentrate on your breathing. Follow your breath inward. Hold for five seconds and relax. Breathe out and release all tension. Focus on the middle of your chest.

In front of you, a golden staircase descends into the earth. Relax as you walk down the ten healing steps to a magical, amethyst crystal cave. Each step immerses you in a quality of compassion. Kindness, sensitivity, sympathy, listening, respect, empathy, caring, distress tolerance, non-judgement and forgiveness.

When you arrive at the crystal cave, find a comfortable place to sit. Imagine the beautiful rose from the image gently floating before you, emitting colourful rays that bathe you in compassion. Imagine inhaling the colour rays through your nose and exhaling them through your mouth.

The colours of compassion fill you and begin to radiate from you, showering the cave with loving kindness. Visualise this loving kindness moving outwards in concentric circles towards all you love — people, animals, places or objects. Continue radiating compassion to all you know and those you do not know. Feel your loving kindness encircling your suburb, city, state, country and the entire world. You are connected to all through your rose of compassion. Feel this connection for as long as you like — at least thirty seconds.

Walk to the golden staircase. As you ascend, pull the concentric circles of compassion back towards you and your heart. Bring this compassion with you as you move back into daily life. Thank your shadow for illuminating the extraordinary ways compassion manifests in the world. When you reach the top of the stairs, take two deep breaths and open your kind and loving eyes.

Inspired Insights, Reflections and Actions

- Open your mind and heart to unlimited compassion. Now imagine they are closed to compassion. What feels different?
- Use compassion to set boundaries. See how compassion protects and balances your precious energy.
- Practise mindfulness. Observe and shift your thoughts to a non-judgemental, loving perspective.
- Witness your emotional responses to the feelings of others so you can provide an unconditional space for them to move forwards with hope.

Journal Work

Write yourself a letter. Take the perspective of a compassionate friend and speak to yourself with their voice. Ask yourself, "What would a compassionate and kind friend say to me right now?"

Once you have finished, don't re-read the letter until 24 hours have passed. When the time comes to read it, open your heart to accept the words with compassion.

16. FORGIVENESS

Release Resentment to Regain Balance

It is time to forgive yourself, a person or a situation. Something has you shackled to anger and resentment. Free yourself so you can welcome healing. Holding someone, perhaps yourself, forever accountable does not right the wrongs of the past. Forgiveness doesn't pardon hurtful behaviour, but it can release you from being disempowered whenever you think or talk about it. You are losing energy that can charge your desires. Reclaim this energy by changing the narrative. Break the pattern and open a door to your dreams. Forgiveness will expand your awareness, vibration, love and trust. It also graces you with choice and improves your wellbeing. Lighten your load so you can jump higher and breathe deeper.

Shadow Mastery Class: Reclaim Your Precious Energy

Meditation

Place a hand on the card. Gently close your eyes. Sense your body and concentrate on your breathing. Follow your breath inward. Hold for five seconds and relax. Breathe out and release all tension. Focus on the middle of your chest.

In front of you, a golden staircase descends into the earth. Relax as you walk down ten healing steps to a magical, amethyst crystal cave. With each step, you are further immersed in forgiveness.

When you arrive at the crystal cave, find a comfortable place to sit. The beautiful heart rose floats in front of you. Focus on the middle of the rose. The rose grows larger, drawing you into its centre.

Now, bring to mind someone you want to forgive; it could even be you. See this person floating in front of you. Harmonious rays of golden light connect you. Focus on the words or actions to be forgiven. Breathe in the memory of the moment and let it be fully present within you. Notice and name your feelings as you relive the hurt.

You may never know what compelled the person to act or speak in a way that hurt you. That is okay. For now, imagine seeing the rift through their eyes. Observing their perspective doesn't mean you agree with it, nor does it absolve them of responsibility, but it may provide some clarity.

When you are ready, give the person a hug and feel the flow of forgiveness release any resentment or anger between you. Affirm to the person, "I am responsible for my consciousness and energy. Forgiveness allows beauty and value to arise from our experience."

Allow the person to simply disappear from view.

Turn to see a mirror on the wall of the cave. Within it, there is a guide or teacher — this is your higher guidance. Ask them, "Have I truly forgiven?" If they say no, repeat this meditation tomorrow.

Whatever the answer, return to the golden staircase. As you ascend, imagine the heart rose embracing you. It will be a shield until you heal. Thank the person or event for giving you the opportunity to know and love yourself in new ways. At the top of the stairs, take two deep breaths and open your wise eyes.

Inspired Insights, Reflections and Actions
Where there is love and balance, there is no need for forgiveness. Resentment and bitterness can arise from judgement, a lack of empathy or emotional pain that keeps us tied to the past. Not forgiving can be a hurdle to spiritual growth and manifesting desires. You can forgive and free yourself from anything.

Journal Work
Write down or draw one thing you want to forgive. Look at the event as you would if a toddler, kitten or puppy broke something dear to you. They may become scared or upset by your disappointment or anger. Perhaps you no longer have those feelings. Instead of a need to forgive, you are likely to understand and reassure them. Write down or draw how you can understand and comfort the person you want to forgive.

17. REIMAGINE

Define Who You Are, Create Who You Want to Be

It is time to reimagine the stories you tell yourself. Ask yourself, "Where do I want to direct my life? What do I want to achieve?" By asking these questions, you consciously shape your destiny, refining and clarifying your highest path. You can begin at any time, and there is no right way to start. You may wish to take charge of your work life, relationships, hobbies or education. There may be an area of your life that feels unfulfilled, a dream that seems unsatisfied or a skill that is yet unrealised. Where you begin your reimagining is up to you. Over the next few days, practice visualising what you would like to experience. Let these visions guide your conscious actions. Your imagination is in an intimate co-creative dance with your soul. Dream and become your future. Shine your imagination and let it light the way.

Shadow Mastery Class: Reconstruct Your Story

Meditation

Place a hand on the card. Gently close your eyes. Sense your body and concentrate on your breathing. Follow your breath inward. Hold for five seconds and relax. Breathe out and release all tension. Then focus on the middle of your chest.

In front of you, a golden staircase descends into the earth. Relax as you walk down the ten healing steps to a magical, amethyst crystal cave. Each step opens your senses to infinite possibilities that spark your imagination. Step into the amethyst cave and greet your shadow.

In front of you, a curtain of light leads to your reimagining room. Walk through the curtain and enter. You are surrounded by a quantum field of all the possibilities that await your creative instruction. You can build anything here, from an experience to a new planet or world. Let your imagination loose. There is no judgement.

Reimagine as many experiences as you like. Create new chapters, asides and characters and let them lead you to surprising possibilities. Whatever unfolds, see yourself thriving and deeply fulfilled through all your experiences. You are so much more than you think you are. Visualise the sights, sounds and smells of your creations. Imagine how your body feels. Enjoy how you feel in each scenario — calm, safe and at peace with yourself and all things. Stay in this space for as long as you like — at least thirty seconds.

Move through the curtain of light and return to the amethyst cave. Walk to the golden staircase. As you ascend, know you can create anything in your mind and life. Thank your shadow for the dark, velvety matrix of possibilities from which you can build a fulfilling future. At the top of the stairs, take two deep breaths and open your eyes to inspiration.

Inspired Insights, Reflections and Actions
When you don't direct your energy, someone or something else will. Commit to your dreams and desires but allow your approach to be flexible and creative. Allow each step to lead to the next. Research positive disintegration, a theory about transformation conceived by psychologist and psychiatrist Kazimierz Dąbrowski.

Journal Work
Think of a scene from your life that you'd like a chance to do over. Reimagine this scene and write or draw about it unfolding in a way that nurtures and empowers the characters. For example, if someone was rude to you and you were rude in return, you might write or draw yourself responding with calm and compassion. You might imagine yourself walking away and focusing your energy on something you enjoy. In this reimagining, you choose how you want to feel. Creating new ways to experience a scene gives you practised strategies for the next time it happens.

18. SURRENDER

Let Your Soul Wisdom Lead the Way

You have been trying to control a situation or force a desired outcome. You are scared of what may happen if you let go and trust the Universe to guide you. However, surrender allows dreams to fall into the elegant love of your soul's wisdom so they can grow. At first, letting go may feel uncomfortable, but it is less painful than what brought you here. Yes, stepping into the unknown can trigger unpleasant emotions, but the energy of surrender will embrace you in grace. It transports you beyond space and time so you can see, feel and think about things differently. Move beyond the obvious and assumed, and relax into your soul's perspective. From this elevated outlook, you will be able to consider all that is beneath, above and surrounding your present circumstances — and fresh energies, opportunities, inspirations and answers will magically appear.

Shadow Mastery Class:
Surrender and Elevate Your Outcomes

Meditation

Place a hand on the card. Gently close your eyes. Sense your body and concentrate on your breathing. Follow your breath inward. Hold for five seconds and relax. Breathe out and release all tension. Focus on the middle of your chest.

In front of you is a descending golden staircase. Walk down the ten healing steps to a magical, amethyst crystal cave. As you move down the steps, think of something you would like to surrender. It might be a person, situation, thought, habit or place. When you arrive at the bottom, step into the amethyst cave and greet your shadow.

A door materialises in front of you. On it, the word 'Surrender' lights up in neon like on a stage door. You open the door and step into a room with no floor. You cling to the doorway until you hear a voice from within say, "Let go. You are safe."

You let go and begin to float. You feel supported and excited. Become the observer and let the scene unfold.

Whatever you have chosen to surrender floats in front of you. It is connected to you by a thick rope. You clutch the rope as if your life depends on it. You may have invested a lot of time and energy in whatever is at the other end of the rope, and it didn't work out the way you thought. It didn't make you happy or make life easier. Feel the pain in your hands as they grip the rope. The need to hang on feels familiar. Your mind says, "Who will I be if I'm no longer clinging to this? What will happen if I let go?"

Your grip tightens, and you are unwilling to let go.

Take a breath, become the observer again and give yourself

permission to surrender. Begin to lift your fingers from the rope, one at a time. Watch as the rope leaves your hands, and all the pain and restriction floats away with it. Wish it well on its new journey. You feel a release, like a weight has been lifted from your shoulders. Stay here for as long as you like — at least thirty seconds.

Float back through the stage door into the amethyst cave. Return to the golden staircase. As you ascend, surrender to your soul wisdom and aim to let the moment inspire your next steps. Thank your shadow for alerting you to the illusion of control. When you reach the top of the stairs, take two deep breaths and open your eyes to freedom.

Inspired Insights, Reflections and Actions

When you surrender, you don't stop creating and directing your life, and you certainly don't let go of your dreams and desires. You merely say goodbye to resistance. When you let go of anything, your consciousness or awareness expands into fresh understanding, and you heighten your perspective. It's impossible to know how everything will play out. Surrender this need and come back to the now. This is where empowerment exists.

Try this exercise: Close your eyes, place your hands at your heart and agree to feel life as it is. Engage your senses. What are you feeling, hearing, smelling, tasting and seeing (behind your closed eyes) right now? Surrender into all that you feel. Breathe deeply three times and open your eyes.

Journal Work

Write down or draw two hurts or habits you would like to surrender. For each hurt or habit, ask the following questions, then write down or draw any information you receive:

- How is this benefiting or serving me?
- How would I feel without this in my life?

At the beginning of every month or the new moon, repeat this exercise with two new things you would like to surrender.

19. ENDINGS

A Natural Progression for Expansion of the Soul

Everything eventually dies. Death is not terrible, a punishment or in opposition to life. It allows new life to flow into existence. Embrace death as a part of life by dying before you die. In this way, you are encouraged to embrace life. What thoughts, behaviours or patterns would instantly fall away if death was imminent? You could begin to experience your best, most fulfilling and desired life by releasing them now. Are you compromising yourself because you don't want something to end? This approach to life can create anxiety around failure or new experiences. It is always unrewarding as you can miss the meaning and magic of life. Embrace an ending and step into the fullness of life by finding gratitude and wonderment in all you have accomplished and created. It is time to release and honour all you have done. As soon as you accept an ending, you can move ahead to create and accomplish more.

Shadow Mastery Class: Embracing Impermanence

Meditation

Place a hand on the card. Gently close your eyes. Sense your body and concentrate on your breathing. Follow your breath inward. Hold for five seconds and relax. Breathe out and release all tension. Focus on the middle of your chest.

Imagine a descending golden staircase before you. Relax as you walk down the ten healing steps to a magical, amethyst crystal cave. Each step aligns you with your higher self or soul, which is eternal and infinite.

Step into the amethyst cave and greet your shadow. In front of you is a doorway with 'Beyond' written above it. As you walk through the opening, you begin to glow. Look down at your hands — can you see them shine? Even if your physical form is different, you will always recognise yourself.

In your glowing state, imagine you are standing in a beautiful forest in autumn. Observe the deciduous trees and the transformation of the leaves. A gentle breeze rustles the leaves and shifts the knowing in your heart. Thank the leaves for their wisdom. The time is ripe for a leaf to release itself from a tree. It has been fed, nurtured and sustained, but it will only transform when it lets go. It frees itself from the tree and drifts like a feather to the waiting arms of Mother Earth. She welcomes the brave leaf into the eternal, loving embrace of all. Here the leaf becomes part of the rich soil where new seeds are planted and grown. Imagine you are that brave leaf sinking into the arms of Mother Earth. Sense how safe and free you feel. You are in a space between chapters of your life, teetering on something new.

Mother Earth gently lifts the changed you back into the amethyst cave. Return to the golden staircase. As you ascend, any fear of death falls away like a leaf. You are ready to move on from your previous experiences and creations. Allow a chapter of your life to end — turn the page and let it be. Say to your shadow, "Thank you for holding my fear of death. Today, I have faced death and learned to embrace life. The fear has disappeared, so there is nothing left for you to hold."

When you reach the top of the stairs, you understand the beauty of life and death. Take two deep breaths in and out, and open your eyes to your glorious life.

Inspired Insights, Reflections and Actions

We can live about a month without food and a few days without water, but only minutes without oxygen. Consider doing the following:

- Honour your body and the breath of life by breathing deeply and consciously.
- Take a walk in a graveyard and thank all who came before you for paving the way so that you can live.
- Discuss death with your friends and family.

Journal Work

Write a list or draw fifty or so things you would like to experience. Go wild! All are accepted. Nothing is too small or big.

This list is a living document. What you desire will change. Tomorrow, you may want something new. Add or remove items at will and check your list every month to see if everything is still relevant.

Remember, no topics are prohibited. You may like to keep this document to yourself. Others don't see with your eyes. If someone misunderstands or reacts adversely, doubt may cloud your desires. If this happens, don't worry. Relax and focus on the deliberate creator you are becoming.

20. 2020 VISION

A New Earth Begins

Clear sight or clairvoyance is ushering in new perspectives and ways to experience life. This time may be challenging as significant change is often preceded by upheaval. Continue along the pathway being revealed to you. There are better times ahead. Avoid looking back and lamenting the closed door of the past, as it may tie you to suffering and regret. Instead, extract the wisdom from your past and project it forwards. Use it to help you restructure your inner and outer boundaries. Make space here, in the present, to rearrange your priorities and imagine how different approaches could play out. Be still, engage your visionary self, and gaze into the periphery of your circumstance. Consider what you may have bypassed by trying to skip ahead without processing life's lessons. Face, embrace and integrate your experiences as wisdom.

Otherwise, they can remain issues that become obstacles to your fulfilment. When everything seems to have turned upside down, engage your 2020 vision for a kinder vision for the future.

Shadow Mastery Class:
Find a Fresh Approach

Meditation

Place a hand on the card. Gently close your eyes. Sense your body and concentrate on your breathing. Follow your breath inward. Hold for five seconds and relax. Breathe out and release all tension. Focus on the middle of your chest.

In front of you is a descending golden staircase. Walk down the ten healing steps to a magical, amethyst crystal cave. Greet your shadow as it emanates from a door in front of you. This door has layers of light depicting the symbol on the card. This imagery connects to the Mayan calendar and the I Ching and represents ways to measure changes in time. Take a breath and float through the door as if you are moving through many dimensions of space and time.

Instead of entering a room, you find yourself floating in front of a wormhole. You see it snaking through space and wonder where it will take you. The words 'Create Thyself' stream through the light that pours from this secret passageway. Everything behind you is history, and everything in front of you is a mystery. You are here, now, on the crest of a soul light wave, about to ride for the sheer joy of it. Jump into the wormhole. You are safe.

Colours rush past as you feel the pull of your soul, and yet you feel like you are still. Look at your hands and see them becoming light. They are glowing. You are vibrating, transforming. The old is peeling away to reveal the magnificence of your soul. This is not a time for returning home, for wherever you are, you are home.

Through the colours of your wormhole, a pulsing star rushes towards you. It fills your vision and embraces you as you journey from the wormhole into the star. Serene, misty energy floats around you. You are suspended in love, deep in the creative heart of the Universe, and it wants to share a message with you. Listen with your heart. Stay here for as long as you like — at least thirty seconds.

You are the centre of your own universe. It is time to create your world instead of living in someone else's. Each moment, each breath, is an opportunity to begin again. Your heart and the creative heart of the Universe have become one. Now focus on your heart space as you float through the multidimensional door into the amethyst cave.

Return to the golden staircase. As you ascend, allow your consciousness to flow from your heart and expand into every cell within your body. Ground all your experiences into your physical self. Thank your shadow for being the gateway to other dimensions. When you reach the top of the stairs, take two deep breaths and open your eyes. Creation awaits.

Inspired Insights, Reflections and Actions

The shadow can resist change in many ways. It might reject the reality before you and suggest or be drawn to alternatives. These theories might not be based on fact but assumption and strung together to fit a specific agenda — such as a less uncomfortable reality. Let alternative views and conspiracy theories activate questions that will find a solution instead of triggering blame or encouraging ignorance.

Many years ago, I attended a lecture by the late writer and teacher Stuart Wilde, who I found engaging and kind, if not a little mischievous. He said something akin to, "If the government was to start taxing air, we would learn to breathe differently." Anything is possible if you believe it.

Consider that whatever you are asked to do is neither good nor bad. How you feel about it determines its effect on you.

Journal Work

Write or draw about an experience or time when you felt isolated or overwhelmed. It could have forced you to change or live differently. To gain deeper information, write or draw about the experience from the perspective of an animal or object that was significant during that time.

- What did you gain?
- What did you lose?
- What did you learn about yourself?
- What did you learn about your friends and family?
- What changes, big or small, did you notice? Or are you still noticing?
- What surprised you?

21. WORLD SHADOW

Veiled Desires are Reawakening

The problems of the world can feel overwhelming. They can also inspire new ways to live, work and play that harmonise with yourself, other humans, animals and nature. Rather than being weighed down by problems, shift your focus and become part of the uplifting solution. Your shadow uses the world shadow to highlight the unfair stories you store from your culture and life. Clarify how you want to live in this world and allow others to live in the world they choose. You have access to the fantastic ideas and creations that swirl in the collective consciousness through your imagination. When you feel things are too much, it means you doubt your ability or worthiness to manifest your dreams and desires. The world loves you and your desires. Relax, breathe and bring those dreams into the light.

Shadow Mastery Class: Change How You See the World, and the World You See Will Change

Meditation

Place a hand on the card. Gently close your eyes. Sense your body and concentrate on your breathing. Follow your breath inward. Hold for five seconds and relax. Breathe out and release all tension. Focus on the middle of your chest.

In front of you is a descending golden staircase. Relax as you walk down the ten healing steps to a magical, amethyst crystal cave. Each step aligns you with your dreams and desires for the world.

Step into the amethyst cave and greet your shadow. In front of you is a mirrored door with 'Your World' written on it. Observe your reflection in the door and notice that 'Your World' is written across your heart. The door opens into a dark circular room. As you enter the room, you begin to float. The darkness is punctuated by twinkling stars and a beautiful, pale blue dot you recognise as Earth. It grows larger to become a beautiful green and blue sphere that you can hold in your hands.

Rays of healing golden light begin to engulf the sphere. It dawns on you that they flow from your third eye and heart. Your higher wisdom is showing you Earth's truth through the mystical eye of unconditional love. You can now see life on Earth through the devotion of Gaia, the consciousness of Earth.

Send golden healing rays of light anywhere or to anyone on Earth. Do this for at least thirty seconds. When you have finished, release Earth from your hands and float towards the open door. Turn around to look at the mirrored door. The writing has changed. Across your heart, it now says, 'You are the World, and the World is You'.

Return to the amethyst cave. Walk to the golden staircase. As you ascend, you feel a full acceptance of your mind, body and spirit fill every cell that makes up your physical body. Thank your shadow for projecting any uncomfortable views you held about yourself upon the world. This coping mechanism was initiated to create balance until you were ready to heal the imbalanced views. When you reach the top of the stairs, you understand the difference between inclusion and acceptance and vow to embrace all things beyond judgement. Take two deep breaths and open your eyes to a beautiful world.

Inspired Insights, Reflections and Actions

When you push something away, it will follow you and show up as unpleasantness in your world. Change needs to begin within you, not out in the world. The physical experience of Earth creates a platform of reality from which life can be explored. You came to Earth knowing life here would offer many opportunities to create bigger experiences and new paths. All experiences, good or bad, will expand you, your world and the Universe.

Free will is about choice. How will you choose to see the events in your life today?

Journal Work

Write down or draw three things that make you sad about the world. Write about or draw how your sadness inspires a new path towards happiness and freedom for you, others and Earth.

22. WORRY

The Illusion of Control

Your concerns for the future are blinding you to the wonderment in your life today. In an effort to feel safe in the present, you seek to control the outcomes of the future. Trauma or a series of hurts may have caused you to become hypervigilant. When we are young, we seek safety. In a chaotic environment, we look to adults or social groups to learn how to feel safe. Many of us were not taught or encouraged to process unsafe feelings. Thus, they move into the shadow and can become unhealthy coping strategies. You may think you will feel safe if you can ensure everyone is okay and everything is done. And that only then will you be worthy enough to create and live your dreams. But there will always be things that are out of your control. Your worries for the future have been trying to keep you safe. They have gotten you here.

Thank them for their support, but it is now time to heal and step into the future with confidence.

Shadow Mastery Class: The Gift of Foreboding

Meditation

Place a hand on the card. Gently close your eyes. Sense your body and concentrate on your breathing. Follow your breath inwards. Hold for five seconds and relax. Breathe out and release all tension. Focus on the middle of your chest.

In front of you is a descending golden staircase. Relax as you walk down the ten healing steps to a magical, amethyst crystal cave. Each step reveals a hurt that triggers worry. Welcome this information as empowering and helpful.

Step into the amethyst cave and greet your shadow. In front of you is a door painted in your favourite colour. It feels inviting, and you enthusiastically enter the room. It is warm, safe and charming. You lie down and sink into a thick, soft carpet. Soft rays of sunlight fill the space, and you begin to see words appearing on the walls, the gifts of your worry.

You might see phrases like "heightened situational awareness", "planning", "security", "structure", "discipline", "protection of loved ones", "habits and routines", "the safety and comfort of others," and "creative solutions." These words represent coping strategies you have in place to keep you and your loved ones safe. As you begin to use these strategies more consciously, you will create a life of unconditional freedom instead of a life of conditions. How many more gifts can you identify? Spend as much time honouring yourself as you wish — at least thirty seconds.

Feel your confidence rise as ways to heal your hurts enter your mind. Let them flow, and know that more will come to you over the following days and weeks. Stand up and move towards the door. Take the wonderment of your creative self with you as you step into the amethyst cave.

Move through the cave to the golden staircase. As you walk upward, thank your shadow for the gift of worry. It has served you in ways that will make you a better person. The next time you experience worry, you will have a better understanding of its purpose. You will also have tools to separate you from your worries in a peaceful way. When you reach the top of the stairs, take two deep breaths in and out and open your eyes to freedom.

Inspired Insights, Reflections and Actions

To live in the moment is to live your truth. Empowerment exists right here and right now. Worry cannot exist when you are fully present in each moment. Learn from the past, plan for the future, act and live now.

You may be aware of your worry, but until you do something different, the knowledge will just feel like a burden. Tools give you different experiences and choices that open paths to freedom. The journal work below is a good place to start.

If your worry feels overwhelming, and it feels safe to do so, close your eyes and take four slow, deep breaths. Breathe in the word 'peace' or 'bliss' and breathe out the word 'safe' or 'secure'. Do this until you feel more relaxed, about five cycles, and then open your eyes.

Journal Work

Create two sections in your journal, one called 'Gratitude' and the other, 'Worries'. Write or draw five things you are grateful for in your gratitude list every day. Add to the list whenever you want.

Throughout the day, check how you are feeling by considering your emotions at that time. If you recognise anything that activates worry, add them to your worries list. Then reflect on your gratitude list or take a few minutes to consider what feels good right now. This tool can help you centre your energy in the moment. You can choose to care about how you feel and delegate time to acknowledge and explore any issues that trigger worry.

Allocate fifteen minutes a day to problem-solving your triggers. During this time, ruminate and devise ways to address the triggers and lessen your worry.

How to problem solve:
1. Explore the cause of the problem.
2. Brainstorm — think about possible solutions.
3. Choose a solution.
4. Plan how to implement the solution.

23. TRIGGERS

Intense Emotional Catalyst

There are areas in our lives that we are good at and others that we have mastered. But there will also be some areas that we find challenging. They might even push our stress buttons and knock us off-centre. Whenever a painful thought or experience is unhealed, it can create an imbalance. This wound will be stored in the shadow and become a body memory. When a similar vibration, situation or experience arises, the wound is poked and can trigger a reaction. We might feel as if our buttons have been pushed. The situation may feel wrong because it hurts, but the pain is telling you something remains unhealed. When we have big buttons out there to be pushed, it's easier for them to be pushed. You may sometimes find yourself thinking that someone knew just the words or behaviours that would upset you, so it is their fault that you reacted as you did. Even when someone deliberately pushes buttons, our response is our responsibility. When you feel your reaction may be bigger than a current situation, it may be linked to stored pain. Take a moment and put some space between you and the emotion for a more empowered response. Later, reflect on the words, behaviours and feelings to discover the wounding and begin the healing process.

Shadow Mastery Class: Pushing Buttons is Fun

Meditation

Place a hand on the card. Gently close your eyes. Sense your body and concentrate on your breathing. Follow your breath inward. Hold for five seconds and relax. Breathe out and release all tension. Focus on the middle of your chest.

Before you, a golden staircase descends into the earth. Walk down the ten healing steps to a magical, amethyst crystal cave. Each step moves you into a calm and centred inner space so you can observe triggers without reacting. Step into the amethyst cave and greet your shadow. In front of you is a large round, blue and purple door. In the middle of the door is a triangle that says 'Push Me'. You tentatively push the button, and the door swings open.

As you step into this room, you are confronted by buttons of all colours and sizes covering the walls. Out of nowhere, a piece of paper whooshes into the room and lands in your hands. You open the paper and read:

When others trigger or push your buttons, you react because they have touched a wound. A hurt or sensitivity has been revealed. Your emotional response can lead you to a pain you have yet to heal. An extreme reaction may be an attempt to protect you from further pain. However, unless you become more open to engaging with and understanding the source of your reaction, the imbalance will remain, and the wound will become bigger and cause more pain each time someone touches (or comes close to) the subject. In this space, you can push as many buttons as you like. As you do so, you will feel a familiar sensation, followed by insight into the wounding you have touched upon. You can choose to press one, none, or many buttons. It is up to you.

And poof! The paper whooshes up and disappears. Decide whether to accept this mission to discover more of yourself. Should you choose not to go ahead, thank the room for the opportunity and know you can return at any time. If you feel prepared to do so, choose a button and start pressing!

When you press a button, the sensations that arise are so real, and the messages that accompany them activate insightful moments of "aha!" This is a thrilling, playful and safe way to engage with reactions you may otherwise find uncomfortable or confronting. The buttons may prompt excitement, anger, hurt, inspiration, fear, annoyance, frustration or love. Have fun observing all the ways you react. You are awakening to a broader version of yourself. The more you work and heal your tender spots, the more open you are to the higher dimensions of soul information. Whether you have chosen to push any buttons or not, stay in the room for as long as you like — at least thirty seconds.

When you are ready, step out of your button room into the amethyst cave. Skip up to the golden staircase. As you ascend, feel empowered and quietly confident that you can recognise when something has touched on a wound and can respond with care and insight. The next time this happens, you will be alert to the lesson and opportunity for self-understanding and growth. Thank your shadow for making you aware of all you are yet to love about yourself. At the top of the stairs, take two deep breaths and open your eyes to wonderment.

Inspired Insights, Reflections and Actions
Consider the ways you can respond to a wound being activated. Contemplate whether the following may be helpful strategies.

- Reflect on whether there is any benefit to feeling the pain of an activated trigger. It may draw your awareness to something or motivate you to make a change.
- Leave the situation. I find taking a toilet break can help. It stops the escalation of the hurt, and you can bring yourself back to a centred, calm mind.
- Acknowledge your emotions without acting on them. Notice your feelings and examine them at an appropriate time. You may wish to add to your list of worry triggers (see *Journal Work* for Card 22).

Journal Work
Write or draw a list of situations, words or behaviours that activate an extreme emotional response for you. Next to each item, write or draw a strategy you can apply to help you find balance. The goal is not to eliminate but to grow awareness of your triggers so you can calm and redirect your reactions, feelings and emotions.

24. DEFENCE MECHANISMS

Soothe Uncomfortable Situations or Thoughts

You are holding emotions and reactions at bay, distracting yourself from the reality they alert you to. Instead of accepting their invitation to acknowledge and address your pain, doubt or fear, you ignore, dull or push them aside. There are many paths of distraction, including food, work, shopping, socialising or over-committing. While it's okay to pursue any of these activities, when we use them to keep ourselves from thinking about difficult situations or feelings, they can become habits or defence mechanisms. Avoidance can even lead to addiction. What may have begun as a coping strategy or process to help you through a problem can become more demanding. This card asks you to consider whether you are giving an activity, person or interest more and more to get you through the day. When this is the case, the activity may be covering over emotions or reactions or keeping your mind too busy to process and find balance within. Our hurts have a way of pushing upward, and something wants to be accepted and released. A mechanism or strategy that was adopted to keep you safe has become a barrier to your best life. Go within, claim your wound, find your pathway to healing and know balance.

Shadow Mastery Class: Create Loving Boundaries

Meditation

Place a hand on the card. Gently close your eyes. Sense your body and concentrate on your breathing. Follow your breath inward. Hold for five seconds and relax. Breathe out and release all tension. Focus on the middle of your chest.

In front of you, a golden staircase descends into the earth. Walk down the ten healing steps to a magical, amethyst crystal cave. As you move down the steps, you begin to let your guard down. There is no judgement here, so there is nothing to protect yourself from; you are safe. When you arrive at the bottom, step into the magical, crystal amethyst cave and greet your shadow.

You are immediately met by a huge wall. It spans out in all directions, and you can't see how to move past it. It is time to dismantle the wall. It has helped you for a long time but has now outlived its usefulness.

Begin to see the wall dissolving. With it, all outdated or limiting strategies, mechanisms, habits and protection also fall away. As they break down, more and more light flows to you.

Numerous colours filled with different vibes and qualities of love, joy and wisdom dance around you. Each breath brings them closer. Allow them to flow in and around you. Draw them deeper and deeper. Fill your body, heart, mind and soul. You have been holding yourself from your truth for so long that this feels like a vibrant new discovery — a free, more empowered you is revealed. Stay with this vision for as long as you like — at least thirty seconds.

It is time to place circles of light around you to create new boundaries. Put divine white light closest to your body to keep your vibration aligned with your soul and heart love. Surround that with intuitive purple to keep you connected to your divine wisdom. Embrace that in communicative blue to help you be open to divine messages for living your best life. Hug that in healing green to be in the vibration of unconditional love. Then enfold that with confident yellow to esteem and trust your inner voice. Cuddle that with emotional orange to clarify the relationships and creativity that is true for you. Finally, wrap everything in the safety and stability of red. Stay with this vision of being safe and empowered by healthy boundaries for as long as you like — at least thirty seconds.

Return to the golden staircase. As you ascend, know these boundaries will be here as long as you need them. Think of them as shields that allow you to clean up your energy so you can live to your potential. The circles of light will naturally fall away when you no longer need them. Thank your shadow for creating mechanisms that kept you safe until you were ready to establish supportive boundaries. At the top of the stairs, take two deep breaths and open your eyes to a confident new you.

Inspired Insights, Reflections and Actions

Defence mechanisms can be a response to discomfort or trauma. They shield us so we can get on with our daily lives. So, they help us to cope. As we discover and understand our discomforts and traumas, we can begin to heal and transform mechanisms into strategies that support balance and productivity. Begin your healing process by nurturing feelings of safety and setting loving boundaries. Creating strategies that move you beyond defensiveness can prompt profound transformation. There is no need to actively eliminate unhelpful defence mechanisms. They will naturally fall away as you focus on more effective and supportive strategies.

Try this: Create an empowerment circle.

- Draw an imaginary circle on the floor at least one metre or yard in diameter.
- Fill it with a colour that makes you feel joyful and empowered.
- Step into the middle of your circle. Take a deep breath and feel exultant and empowering vibrations inspire a new sense of confidence.
- While still in your circle, think of one thing you have done well. (Use a different accomplishment each time you use this technique.)
- Stay here for as long as you like and enjoy the feeling.
- When you have finished, step out of the circle.
- Imagine picking up your circle and placing it in your heart.
- Use this strategy whenever you would like to boost your esteem or override a defence mechanism.

Journal Work

Choose a challenging experience and draw or write about how it made you a better person. Then write down or draw the boundaries you will put in place to support you in preventing or responding to similar situations. Knowing you have the tools to respond to difficult situations will help you expand your world and grow into your potential.

25. STRESS

Freedom from Fight, Flight and Freeze

Left unattended, tension can build until even minor upsets can be stressful. When your body can't distinguish between real or imagined danger, it reacts with a cocktail of hormones that create the fight, flight or freeze stress response. This helps your body stay focused, energetic and alert. However, this reaction is meant to be reserved for quick fixes and short-term use. It is first aid for stress, not for ongoing application. Ideally, once the feeling of immediate danger has passed, your body will switch to a neutral state so recovery and healing can begin. It is easier to identify the stresses from the outside world than those of your inner world. Whether your stress is inwards or outwards, the result is the same. You can't change what happens around you, but you can choose how to respond. Care about how you feel and focus on calm.

Shadow Mastery Class: Activate the Relaxation Response

Meditation

Place a hand on the card. Gently close your eyes. Sense your body and concentrate on your breathing. Follow your breath inward. Hold for five seconds and relax. Breathe out and release all tension. Focus on the middle of your chest.

In front of you, a golden staircase descends into the earth. As you walk down the ten healing steps to a magical, amethyst crystal cave, feel your body and mind begin to soften.

Step into the amethyst cave and greet your shadow. Before you is an emerald-green door called 'Tranquillity'. The door quietly opens and invites you in. You feel safe and protected as you enter the room.

You are standing in your ideal place of complete relaxation. Find a place to sit or lie and focus on your breath. A beautiful sense of peace and relaxation moves calmly around and through you. It begins to glow with your favourite colour. Feel a growing sense of peace and relaxation flow over and through you with a gentle warmth, soothing and easy. Sit with this feeling. If you feel yourself becoming restless, imagine turning down the volume on your thoughts. They can be there, but they are not your focus. Let them rise like bubbles and float away.

Continue to breathe deeply and slowly and when you feel ready, scan your body for tension or tightness. If you notice any, observe it without reacting. Just let it be there. One by one, gently breathe into those areas of your body, allowing the wonderful sense of peace and relaxation to embrace and lovingly convert any tension, resistance or pain into softness and ease. As the tight energy loosens, notice any stored emotions and observe your responses to them. You may feel the urge to run from, justify, farewell or embrace the emotion. Accept however you feel and continue to breathe peace and relaxation into the tension until it softens, transforms and releases.

Scan your body until every part of you feels soft and easy. Focus on your breath and imagine it has turned gold. Breathe in gold. Breathe out gold. Imagine your whole being is filled with liquid gold and surrounded by golden stardust. Sit in this golden space for as long as you like — at least thirty seconds.

When you are ready, farewell your tranquillity room and return to the amethyst cave. Thank your shadow for alerting you to your stress so you can activate the relaxation response.

Return to the golden staircase. Complete relaxation and peace accompany you as you ascend the stairs. Feel it flow through your physical body and into your life. Breathe gold in and out as you open your eyes.

Inspired Insights, Reflections and Actions

Trying to think of nothing requires you to engage your thoughts. The concept of clearing the mind is not meant to be taken literally. Rather, it involves allowing thoughts to be present without reaction. Thoughts will arise during meditation or relaxation. By observing them without engagement, judgement or attempting to push them away, your relaxation process can continue and even deepen.

Mindfulness is a mind-focusing technique that can dissolve stress and help you be present in the now. Mindfulness and meditation can also do wonders for productivity, helping you do less and accomplish more. It is like restarting your computer, resetting and bringing things up to date. Any time spent in meditation is helpful — even a couple of minutes. Reducing stress and tension supports physical and emotional healing. Cultivate mindfulness, live mindfully and be more at ease.

Exercise: Find a peaceful space to lie or sit in quiet contemplation. Allow any thoughts and feelings to rise and fall. Observe them without becoming attached. Do this for a few minutes and continue each day for a week or two, gradually increasing the time spent in mindfulness.

Journal Work
Multitasking can scatter energy, thoughts and focus across many areas simultaneously and be a huge stressor. In a relatively short time, overthinking can become habitual and creep into other areas of your life.

Write or draw a list of daily tasks that need to be done. Break them into single tasks and consider whether you can get help with any of them. If you share a household or have people around, doing things together can be fun and bonding. You can also reduce stress by devoting your time to one task at a time. Allow each task to become the inspiration for the next one. Through focus and attention, tasks can be accomplished well in less time. Reflect on the everyday moments where you can find joy. Write about them in your journal to bring feelings of meaning and satisfaction to the simple moments of your life. You might also gift yourself time to immerse yourself in one thing that interests or relaxes you — learn about a crystal, draw a mandala or write a haiku. Record this experience in your journal.

26. SEPARATION

Reconnecting to Your Centre

This card suggests you may feel lost or dissatisfied and can't quite put your finger on what is wrong. When was the last time you consciously connected to your soul's perspective? You may have disconnected from your purpose. This can happen for many reasons, such as disappointment, distress or distraction. You may have lost trust in yourself and be looking for answers from another or the outside world. Lost confidence may mean you are reluctant to make decisions for yourself and are happier to have someone take on that responsibility for you. Self-trust and confidence make up part of our whole self. When they are lost or diminished, we can feel fragmented, our instincts can weaken, and it is easier to veer from our truth and our path. Knowing what you want is part of the process of discovering all of who you are. Creating and respecting your comfort zone can be integral to healing your separation and bringing you home to your soul truth. Thus, establishing and reinforcing boundaries will help you know what feels right for you. You can then navigate challenging situations more purposefully and be excited by possibilities aligned with your soul truth.

Shadow Mastery Class: Claiming Your Wholeness

Meditation

Place a hand on the card. Gently close your eyes. Sense your body and concentrate on your breathing. Follow your breath inward. Hold for five seconds and relax. Breathe out and release all tension. Focus on the middle of your chest.

A golden staircase descends into the earth in front of you. Relax as you walk down the ten healing steps to a magical, amethyst crystal cave. With each step, you become aware of empty parts of yourself that want to be refilled. Step into the amethyst cave and greet your shadow. In front of you is a smooth metal door called 'Retrieval'. It is safe to enter.

You enter the room to find spirals floating in the air around you. These are aspects of yourself that you have separated from. They may have been too painful to integrate in the past, but now you are ready to regain wholeness, and you ask them to gently rejoin you.

Take a breath and feel all of you vibrating in unison. You see the spirals as your soul sees them, and they transform into clouds of dreams and desires that gently move around you. The clouds move and pulse around you with different colours. Feel them as part of you and when you are ready, draw them into yourself and feel spiritually, emotionally and physically whole. Stay here for as long as you like — at least thirty seconds.

Return to the amethyst cave. Thank your shadow for alerting you to the separation that was holding you back. As you ascend the golden staircase, feel grateful for this deeper understanding of yourself. At the top of the stairs, take two deep breaths and open your eyes to wholeness, knowing any sense of separation is an illusion.

Inspired Insights, Reflections and Actions

Your soul has a view of your circumstances that is whole and unconditional. Imagine your circumstances or progress have inspired new desires. When this happens, your soul goes willingly to the desire without judging or trying to figure out how to get it or even if it is worthy. It simply expands into your desire for the bliss of creating. The physical you may not yet be aware of this process. Until you catch up with your expanded consciousness, you may feel a separation — as if something is missing. Stressful events can shatter your sense of harmony and security and make you feel disempowered. However big or small, these events can also create a sense of separation.

- Do you doubt your instincts and regularly ask others for advice, do what they say and then feel dissatisfied or disappointed with the results? When you ask for guidance or advice, listen and take in the information, then let it settle. Sit with the information before making a decision.

- When you feel disconnected, touch your heart. This touchpoint grounds and connects your mind, body and soul to give you access to your soul's wisdom.

Journal Work

Draw or write about a time when you felt disappointed by a choice you made. You might have thought it was the best course of action, but it didn't turn out how you wanted. Now, look at the result. Did it bring clarity about what you did want? When you know what you don't like, it becomes easier to understand what you do want.

Now, draw or write about a time when you felt surprised by how well a choice you made turned out. It might be that a simple or random decision led you to a new friend, discovery or opportunity. However inconsequential the choice felt, let it remind you of the mysterious ways life can unfold when you trust and follow your instincts.

How have these experiences brought more profound clarity to your life?

27. JOURNEY INTO DARKNESS

Know Your Heart and Dreams

To dream is to dare to believe. When you don't believe a desire is within reach, denying or pushing it aside can be a way to avoid disappointment or heartache. This card asks you to reconsider the dreams you have denied yourself. Dare to let them surface. Let them breathe! Perhaps you have sought love and acceptance by living the way someone or society deemed appropriate for you. Your power may be wrapped up in ideas or limitations that are not entirely your own. When dreams are routinely unacknowledged, it creates a pattern of searching outside yourself to feel better, for happiness. In such cases, even when you reach a goal, satisfaction can be fleeting as it does not spring from your authentic self. If this is a long-term pattern, perhaps established in childhood, you may have forgotten how to recognise the call of your dreams. This can seem like being disconnected from your light. Should you feel yourself spiralling or struggling to chase external expectations, gently connect with your heart and honour your feelings. Practice listening to, and making choices from, your authentic self. You can begin with simple things, and as you build confidence in your self-expression, your dreams will sing louder so you can live them prouder. Even though this message is general, reading it will open you to new truths.

Shadow Mastery Class: More Than You Believe You Are

Meditation

This moving meditation will help to shift energetic blocks. You will need a watch or an electronic device to time your movements. Stand up, bend your knees and move your hips in a figure-eight motion eleven times. Pause, then repeat the movement every minute for seven minutes. Try to make the figure-eight a little bigger each time. As you move your hips, feel your energy freeing. Breathe deeply between each round of movement. You may like to sit down at the end of each set and then stand up to begin the next round of eleven movements. When you have completed seven rounds, practise deep breathing for another minute. Pause to reflect on how you feel before beginning the following visualisation.

When you are ready, place a hand on the card. Gently close your eyes. Sense your body and concentrate on your breathing. Follow your breath inward. Hold for five seconds and relax.

Breathe out and release all tension. Focus on the middle of your chest.

In front of you, a golden staircase descends into the earth. Relax as you walk down the ten healing steps to a magical, amethyst crystal cave. Each step unfolds qualities of your soul: appreciation, wisdom and bliss. Accept that these qualities are within you and are emerging.

When you arrive at the amethyst crystal cave, a vast pool of silvery water spreads out before you. Light dances across the pool and over the crystal walls bringing the transformational healing qualities of the cave to life. This is all for you. You are worthy of magic and healing and so very loved.

Notice a white towel on the shore of the healing waters. Remove your clothes and leave them next to the towel. Enter the pool and immerse yourself. The water is calming, cleansing and freeing. You feel so safe within its silvery flow. Become aware of the lightness of your heart as your dreams are released and come to life in the waters.

Be present in whatever you experience within the pool. Stay with the feelings, thoughts, memories or visions that are revealed. Whisper to them, "I believe in you." This is the beginning of a healing process. You may have a physical response, such as laughing or crying. Embrace any reaction you have and go deeper, yet gently, into your process. Go easy on yourself. As you let your dreams be free and seen as they are, you will begin to feel lighter. Healing has begun.

This beautiful space offers a sense of inner knowing and calmness that can only be known from the heart. Layers of conditioned beliefs float away in the waters and are replaced by relief and compassion. Remember the innocent you, who did not yet know disappointment or limitation. Feel yourself floating in creativity, hope and joy. Stay immersed in your pool of light and dreams for as long as you like — at least thirty seconds.

When you are ready, step out of the pool and dry yourself with the warm, fluffy, white towel. A new set of clothes has replaced your old ones. Put them on. They are so comfortable and in your favourite colours.

Return to the golden staircase. As you ascend, feel your dreams and the qualities of your soul journey with you into everyday life. Thank the darkness for illuminating the path back to your heart. At the top of the stairs, take two deep breaths and open your eyes to the possibility that all you desire is possible. In the days that follow, inspired action will come to you.

Inspired Insights, Reflections and Actions
Surrounding yourself with protective layers can shut out the full experience of life. You may not feel the sharpness of disappointment, but your capacity to hope, dream and love will be diminished. This can feel like a generalised dissatisfaction or sadness. Daring to live to fullness does have risks, but you can manage the challenges that will arise, and are ready and deserving of joy.

Things to ponder and try:

- It may feel safer to bury the authentic self to be like everyone else. But what if everyone is burying truth and pretending to be something to fit into an impossible ideal? By choosing to live authentically, you could start a revolution of happiness!
- When you shower or bath, revisit the silvery waters of your healing meditation and let your dreams come to life around you.

Journal Work

When you feel uninspired or down, this exercise is another way to rebalance and understand your feelings. Pause and go within. Write down or draw your feelings in whatever way they want to reveal themselves. Stay with your thoughts, sensations and impressions until you feel there is nothing more to write or draw.

When you have done this a few times, you will begin to see a pattern as the same themes, expressions or feelings will come up repeatedly. The scenario may differ, but how you approach it will be the same. Once you begin to see the pattern in your responses, you can harness the desires, redirect the doubts, transform the fear and dare to believe in your dreams.

Congratulations! You are beginning to reclaim your power.

28. CONFLICT

Know What You Dislike, Focus on Your Likes

A struggle may be threatening your sense of harmony and security. Be alert to manufactured scenarios or the need to prove a point. Pause, centre yourself and choose to be happy over being correct. If you find yourself being pulled into the same old argument or disagreement, ask yourself whether the unpleasantness has an alternative. Try something different, and the outcome might be a scenario that feels better. There may also be times when you are afraid a conflict will compromise your truth, build resentment or limit your choices. Conflict is inevitable as people think, feel and want different things. It is in no way an indication that you are wrong, a failure or being difficult, nor is it a personal slight. Your experience with conflict may be troubled. For example, you may have grown up or worked in an environment where the slightest disagreement could escalate into a high-stakes argument. You may be unsure of how to respond to conflict in a steady, positive manner, so you do your best to avoid it. No outcome is wasted because knowing what you don't want is a big step towards understanding and choosing what you do want. Grow your ability to manage conflict by being aware of how your body reacts. Aim to move from a stress response to a relaxed response so you can remain present. Listen and consider everyone's needs, as well as your own. Get to know your truth.

Shadow Mastery Class: Resolving Inner Conflict

Meditation

Place a hand on the card. Gently close your eyes. Sense your body and concentrate on your breathing. Follow your breath inward. Hold for five seconds and relax. Breathe out and release all tension. Focus on the middle of your chest.

In front of you, a golden staircase descends into the earth. As you walk down the ten healing steps to a magical, amethyst crystal cave, your body relaxes, your mind becomes quiet and peace-loving energy moves around you. Step into the amethyst cave and greet your shadow.

In front of you, a green door labelled 'Conflict Resolution' swings open. Harmonious energy embraces and invites you in. You eagerly move into the room.

The room is bathed in a green light that emulates the energy of nature. You feel at ease and safe. A comfortable armchair beckons you to sit in it. A movie screen drops down. It begins to show a conflict you have with yourself. Listen to the way you speak to yourself. Is this how you would talk to a friend or loved one? The movie screen flashes the words, "Are you willing to be your personal conflict coach?" Yell a big "YES!"

Pause and breathe deeply before saying anything else. Be present with all you are feeling, then scan your body from head to toe, relaxing each part as you go. Regulate your breathing and acknowledge that you have time and space to figure out what you want and to make a choice that makes your soul sing. Challenge any assumptions that arise and respond to any negative self-talk with love and reassurance. This activates your soul's wisdom which projects a resolution to your conflict onto your movie screen. It then shows you a few simple steps for moving forwards. Allow the energy of change to embrace you. Stay here for as long as you like — at least thirty seconds.

Gently arise from your comfortable chair and move back through the green door into the amethyst cave. Return to the golden staircase. As you ascend, notice how confident and peaceful you feel about conflict. You have begun your new relationship with conflict by responding to your inner conflict with calm, love and compassion. Thank your shadow for revealing your conflict with conflicts so you can grow further into your potential. At the top of the stairs, take two deep breaths in and out. Open your peaceful eyes to a new world.

Inspired Insights, Reflections and Actions
When new information challenges our beliefs, we may experience inner conflict. This could be felt as a challenge to our identity or place in the world and accompanied by a heightened emotional response.

Consider and try the following:
- Focusing on blaming yourself or others can be an obstacle to empowered resolutions. Opening a creative dialogue can lead to changed behaviours and solutions.
- Inner conflict tends to cause outer strife and raise tension and stress. Being kinder to yourself and nurturing inner harmony will make the external world a kinder, more peaceful place.

Journal Work
Recall a time in your life when you stood up for yourself. Write or draw about what you did, how you felt and what, if anything, you would do differently.

29. THE BIGGER PICTURE

See All Sides Without Contradiction

Meditation, reading, learning, communication and experience can help us to expand our understanding of a subject, event or situation. Once we have opened ourselves to other views and interpretations, what do we do with that information? A heightened perspective may challenge the idea that everything happens for a reason or that an outcome was fated. These sentiments can feel empty and disempowering when held up to suffering. An expanded awareness can help join the dots and reveal how seemingly random events fit together. However, not everyone will have the same pieces of the puzzle nor be able to see the connections. Everyone is on a unique journey, discovering new elements of life in their own time and pace. When you find an issue challenging, ask for help and be open to broadening your perspective. Your higher self holds your soul truth and will always share higher wisdom that can be integrated into everyday life. Gift yourself time to acquaint yourself with a new perspective. While you wait, send love to the world.

Shadow Mastery Class: Reach Beyond Your View

Meditation

Place a hand on the card. Gently close your eyes. Sense your body and concentrate on your breathing. Follow your breath inward. Hold for five seconds and relax. Breathe out and release all tension. Focus on the middle of your chest.

In front of you, a golden staircase descends into the earth. Walk down the ten healing steps to a magical, amethyst crystal cave. Each step brings a more profound and higher awareness of your physical senses and how they interact and interpret the environment around you. Step into the amethyst cave and greet your shadow.

A nebulous cloud of many colours floats before you. The words 'Gateway to the Bigger Picture' shimmer and shine like golden stars within the cloud. You can already feel yourself expanding. As you walk through the gateway, you expand even further and float and fly through space. You are safe. Enjoy the ride.

Your awareness expands beyond your body. Notice your senses and feelings. Expand your awareness still further and see yourself floating high above Earth. See how peaceful the beautiful blue and green planet looks from your higher perspective.

Expand even further, moving through space, stars and galaxies, expanding into the known universe. Sense the source of all things in your heart sharing information with your soul. Notice what you are feeling and experiencing.

Now, expand beyond the known universe; you are safe to explore uncharted space. You are a pioneer experiencing something no other human has. You are moving to the edge of the worlds to gather information to help you and humanity. You may even inspire others to go on their own journeys. If this great expansion makes you slightly light-headed or overwhelmed, imagine your awareness receding slowly to your comfort zone and then expanding again. Stay in a comfortable, expanded space for as long as you like — at least thirty seconds.

When you feel ready, gently draw your expanded awareness back to the nebulous gateway. You float through into the amethyst cave and reach the golden staircase. As you ascend, allow all you experienced (whether in words, symbols, colours, feelings, knowings or something beyond your comprehension and knowledge) to flow through your awareness into your physical body. Thank the darkness for showing you the eternal reach of space. There is so much space for new creations.

At the top of the stairs, take two deep breaths and open your eyes to an expanded view.

Inspired Insights, Reflections and Actions
All possibilities exist, but what we see and feel of any subject is limited.

Consider and try the following:

- In a difficult situation, try saying: "I don't understand why this is happening, and I wish it wasn't happening to you. Let's just sit here for a while until something comes to us." Something will come. The other person may cry, get angry or just sit in silence; whatever is happening, just let it happen. This is about them, not you!

- In a happy situation, try saying: "I am so glad this is happening for you; let's celebrate."
- Go out on a clear evening, look up to the stars or the moon and imagine what they are looking at.

Journal Work

Draw or write about one thing in your life you truly love. List ten qualities about it you like. Then list ten qualities about it you don't like. They may be harder to find, but everything has positive and negative components. It depends on how you view it.

Next, write down or draw one thing in your life that you truly loathe. List ten qualities about it you dislike. Then list ten qualities about it you like. They may be harder to find, but again, everything has positive and negative components depending on how you look at them.

30. NYCTOPHILIA

Comfort in Darkness

You have found safety in the shadows. You may have diminished yourself to avoid attention. And maybe you have felt invisible or overlooked in conversations and decision-making because no one seems to hear you. Perhaps you have retreated into the background, as observing feels much safer than interacting with others. Are you scared to speak up for fear of ridicule or confrontation? Moving within the darkness can help you be less fearful of the unknown. It can be a place of safety while you study your environment and build your confidence. However, if you flee into darkness, the shadow may obscure the solutions. Imagine yourself as a planted seed. Once it chooses to grow, it moves towards the light. It is time for you to heal and grow by stepping out of the shadows into the sunlight. When you feel pulled to visit the darkness, it is to find harmony and balance within your heart and soul — not to hide from the world. Turn to the light. It's time to grow!

Shadow Mastery Class: Making the Unknown Known

Meditation

Place a hand on the card. Gently close your eyes. Sense your body and concentrate on your breathing. Follow your breath inward. Hold for five seconds and relax. Breathe out and release all tension. Focus on the middle of your chest.

In front of you, a golden staircase descends into the earth. You begin to walk down the ten healing steps to a magical, amethyst crystal cave. With each step, your surroundings become darker and darker until it is so dark that you must feel your way down. When you arrive at the bottom of the steps, a violet glow lights the way to the back of the cave.

In the dim light, you make out a seat carved into the amethyst wall. Move over to it and sit down. Once you are sitting comfortably, all light, sound and smells disappear. It is now so dark that you can't see your hand in front of you. You feel the seat dissolve from beneath you, but you remain supported, comfortable and suspended in the space. There is nothing for your physical senses to notice — no sound, sight, smell, taste or touch. It's like a sensory deprivation tank, except you are floating in a black velvety matrix. The unknown is becoming known as answers begin to form in the innocence of newness. Breathe in freshness and feel how wonderful it is to be at one with yourself and all things. Stay here for as long as you want — at least thirty seconds.

You notice an almost imperceptible point of light pulsing in the distance. As you focus on it, it begins to expand and come closer. The light reveals a new dawn of beauty and harmony. At this moment, you are reborn.

Golden light surrounds you like a gentle mist, lifting and moving you from the back of the cave towards the golden staircase. Floating effortlessly, you ascend the stairs and arrive at the top with a sense of freedom and joy. You now know yourself on a deeper level. Still, you are so much more than you realise. Thank your shadow for enabling the darkness to show you your light.

Gently open your eyes. You are a star!

Inspired Insights, Reflections and Actions
Without the darkness, you would not see the beauty of stars, candle flames or your inner light.

Try the following:

- Put a blindfold on and walk around a familiar room to activate and heighten your other senses.
- When you meditate, imagine inky blackness behind your eyes as a matrix of possibilities and allow fresh ideas to arise.

Journal Work
Night allows us to integrate, clarify and strengthen our daytime experiences. This may happen in dreams or points of realisation that punctuate the darkness as "aha!" moments. In sleep, you let go of conscious thought, so higher messages can flow into your knowing.

Place your journal and a pen next to your bed. When you go

to bed, affirm that you are open to receiving and remembering messages from your soul and soul family. Record any dreams, impressions or thoughts that come to you upon waking.

31. THE WOUNDED CHILD

Healing Trauma Makes the World Feel Safer

Your inner child is the most sensitive, creative and spontaneous you. Sometimes they come looking for love and acceptance. When wounded, your inner child can reach out to you through tantrums, micromanagement, justification, rationalisation or by overexplaining. You might also experience a fear of abandonment, wobbly boundaries or self-doubt. When any of these indicators arise, your inner child wants to be listened to and cared for. Become your inner parent by comforting, protecting and standing up for your wounded child. This self-nurture will foster a sense of security for your vulnerability, innocence and softness. Ask your wounded child what they need and listen with an open heart. You will learn something new about yourself and gain wisdom and guidance. Go gently. Avoid pushing your ideas on them or trying to make them grow up. Rather, have fun with them. The safer and more loved they feel, the more they can heal. Practise seeing everything and everyone through the eyes of your healed child. You are free to create joy and fulfilment from their view of curiosity and wonder.

Shadow Mastery Class: Be the Parent You Always Wanted

Meditation

Place a hand on the card. Gently close your eyes. Sense your body and concentrate on your breathing. Follow your breath inward. Hold for five seconds and relax. Breathe out and release all tension. Focus on the middle of your chest.

In front of you, a golden staircase descends into the earth. Relax as you walk down the ten healing steps to a magical, amethyst crystal cave. With each step, you feel yourself being drawn closer to your heart of fun and joy. Step into the amethyst cave and greet your shadow. In front of you, a bright rainbow rises through the cave. Steps form in the rainbow. Follow them to the top, where a luminous heart materialises in front of you.

Step into the heart. You are safe and cared for. The heart shows you something from your childhood that wants to be healed. As an adult, you have the power to change outcomes. You are magical. Use your superpower of imagination to see the situation or experience playing out differently. See your inner child nurtured, strengthened and healed. From the centre of the healing heart, your inner child skips or runs towards you. Open your arms and embrace them. Whisper into their ear that you will always make a safe space for them to create, play and enjoy. They melt into your arms and then deeper into your heart.

Step out of the heart to the other side of the rainbow, which has turned into a slide. Jump on and begin your slide back to the amethyst cave. Wind rushes past you, and you laugh as you are unceremoniously dumped into the pot of gold at the end of the rainbow slide.

Climb out of the pot of gold and return to the golden staircase. As you ascend, hope, joy and creativity rise with you. Thank your shadow for tending to your childhood wounds until you were ready to heal them. At the top of the stairs, take two deep breaths in and out and open your eyes to spontaneity and fun.

Inspired Insights, Reflections and Actions

You are responsible for being an unconditionally loving parent to your inner child and creating a safe, psychological inner space. Inner child work helps you to understand the foundations that informed your development and any childhood wounds you may have. As an adult, you can deliberately and consciously reshape yourself.

Exercise: Observe younger generations. How are they teaching you to have a better relationship with your inner child?

Once a week, do something you enjoyed as a child, such as eating ice cream, playing a board or video game, colouring in, drawing or writing. You are not being childish but allowing the fun, imaginative inner child to merge with your adult self to create your dream life.

Journal Work

Describe what your inner child looks like with words or drawings. Then invite them to share their wounds. After 24 hours, ask your inner child what you can do or provide to help them heal. This exercise is not about looking for blame in the past but about healing in the now. The environment we grew up in may have included parents, adults or a society that carried wounds they inadvertently pushed upon children. You cannot change what happened, but you can give your inner child the love, care, resources, encouragement and whatever else it needs to grow strong now.

32. THE WOUNDED ADULT

Healing is Feeling

You may have been waiting for someone to believe in your dreams — as if they are not worthy of pursuit until you get the green light from an external party. This doubt dilutes your inner truth, making it feel wishy-washy and far-fetched. Waiting for permission to live can create an unfulfilling environment where sadness, regret and worry can flourish. When you feel down or out of sorts, you begin to focus on yourself. So, in a roundabout way, your pain is bringing you home to yourself, just as insecurities and the need for validation are types of signposts. The discomfort you may be experiencing is due to the gap between the soul's vision and the ego's perspective. The soul sees through unconditional eyes of non-judgement and love. The ego sees through conditional eyes of opinion and fear. Step back and take in both views. Seeing the fuller picture will help balance your perception so healing can begin ... and you can dare to believe in yourself and your dreams, thus reinvigorating hope, passion and enthusiasm for life.

Shadow Mastery Class: Allow Your Heart Rose to Blossom

Meditation

Place a hand on the card. Gently close your eyes. Sense your body and concentrate on your breathing. Follow your breath inward. Hold for five seconds and relax. Breathe out and release all tension. Focus on the middle of your chest.

In front of you, a golden staircase descends into the earth. Relax as you walk down the ten healing steps to a magical, amethyst crystal cave. With each step, feel yourself being drawn closer to your heart rose of healing. Step into the amethyst cave and greet your shadow.

A luminous circular doorway materialises in front of you. It is safe to enter. You step through a curtain of what looks like barbed wire but is soft and bouncy like rubber. You emerge on the other side, into your heart rose.

When you arrived on Earth and opened your heart to life, your soul formed rosebuds waiting to blossom. Some of your rosebuds have blossomed fully, and some you hold tightly closed to protect against pain. Right now, you are ready to awaken your rosebuds and know the absolute fullness of you.

Take a breath and step fully into your heart. Feel your heart's strength, resilience and capacity to forgive and transform. Liberate your heart — feel it expanding to create space for your buds to blossom. Your heart expands to embrace the whole of you.

It expands above, around and below you. You are weightless, suspended in your heart space, surrounded by roses of many colours. Float among the sweet and sensual fragrance they release. Breathe in this fragrance and stay here for as long as you like — at least thirty seconds. All your dreams and desires will be expressed with an open heart.

Move towards the circular door and into the amethyst cave. Return to the golden staircase. As you ascend, become aware of your growing optimism as old hurts fall away. Thank your shadow for protecting your rosebuds until you were ready for them to blossom. You are becoming more of your truth.

At the top of the stairs, take two deep breaths in and out and open your eyes to new beginnings.

Inspired Insights, Reflections and Actions
Try this exercise to soothe wounds:

- Cup your hands at your heart centre.
- Close your eyes and imagine a pink or green rose gently floating in your hands.
- Place your hands and the rose on your body where you feel a wound or hurt.
- Hold your hands in place for three minutes, and imagine your rose embraces the wound with love.
- Feel your hurt fading and a sense of relief wash over you.
- Open your eyes.

Things to try and consider:

- Accept where you are now to allow change to begin. Do not confuse acceptance with forgiveness. Acceptance is required to forgive, but you don't have to forgive to accept.
- When you are integrating new approaches and feel stuck — breathe and wait. Trust that the next steps will soon reveal themselves.
- Buy yourself a bunch of roses and enjoy the healing energy they bring to your environment.

Journal Work
To identify the doubts that hold you from fully living your dreams, write down or draw an event from the past that hurt you. The pain of this event is reactivated each time you think about it or experience a similar situation. Write or draw about how wanting to avoid that pain has influenced your choices. Now write a note thanking your shadow for trying to keep you from pain. Let it know that you are now stronger and wiser and ready to move forwards to the joys awaiting you. Invite it to come along.

33. HEART LOVE

The Unconditional Centre

Outdated ideas about love may be preventing you from seeing the beauty of love all around you. This may be with a lover, partner, child or animal or at home, work or in business. Wherever you are or whoever you are with, you may be unable to see or feel that others are appreciative of you in a loving way. Heart love is unconditional. It is constant and present in all circumstances. As children, we may have learned that we had to be a certain way to be loved — to be something other than our true selves to be worthy. This teaching may not have been conscious or done out of malice. The parents, caregivers or teachers may have felt the same way — disconnected from heart love. Come back to your centre and care about your feelings. Gently refocus on your heart to remember the truth, wisdom and love of you. Heart love recognises something greater in a world of duality and comparison. It sees the beauty in all that you are.

Shadow Mastery Class: Touch Your Heart Love

Meditation

Place a hand on the card and then hold it to your heart. Gently close your eyes. Sense your body and concentrate on your breathing. Follow your breath inward. Hold for five seconds and relax. Breathe out and release all tension. Focus on the middle of your chest.

In front of you, a golden staircase descends into the earth. Give appreciation and thanks to your body, mind and soul for all the unconditional love and support they give, even when you don't recognise it. They walk with you down the ten healing steps and into a magical, amethyst crystal cave.

Find a comfortable place to sit. Gradually, the moon from the card shines light into your inner world to awaken your inner eye and other psychic senses. Bring your attention to the hand on your heart and rest your complete focus on this space of heart love. Notice how easy it feels to focus here.

Misty moonlight drifts around you, drawing you deeper and deeper into your heart love to reveal a hidden temple made of light. The words 'Know Thy Heart' are inscribed above the entrance. Pure loving energy radiates from your temple. Open your heart, mind and body to fully receive the love freely offered to you. You are now floating deep within the consciousness of your heart love.

A special moonlight healing washes over your heart, cleansing, clearing and softening any hard edges. It feels like a gentle vibration pulsing through you. Know yourself as love, for you are becoming your soulmate. Stay here for as long as you like — at least thirty seconds.

Return to the golden staircase. As you ascend, feel your heart love centre in your chest. Thank the darkness for allowing you to see and feel the moonlight that will keep surrounding you as you adjust to the vibration of heart love. At the top of the stairs, take two deep breaths and open your eyes to the love surrounding you. You are love, and you are loved.

Inspired Insights, Reflections and Actions
Wanting unconditional love is conditional. External love isn't the complete remedy for filling an internal emptiness. You may not know how to see, feel or receive love or think you are worthy of it.

Try the following:

- Heart love yourself so you can give and receive unconditional heart love.
- Watch movies or read books with healing, romance, transformation, redemption or adversity as themes to help you feel into the needs of your heart.

Journal Work
Sometime in the next week, take yourself on a date. Do something you have always wanted to do. Don't look to the experience to make you feel good; find a way to feel good beforehand. Take a breath and centre yourself before you go. Your energy will shift into higher vibrations, allowing you to receive even more of your desires and dreams.

This celebration will give you a sense of achievement and empowerment. You don't need anyone else to go out with to experience something you genuinely want to do, see or feel. Don't wait until your birthday to celebrate; instead, make every day a new birthday.

Go for it; celebrate your life.

Write about your date with yourself in your journal. Reflect on the ways you experienced love — both as giver and receiver.

34. INTIMACY SHADOW

Beyond Fear to Connection

Some people seem to flow with the tides as friendships, relationships and lovers move in and out of their lives. For others, being open to intimacy can take courage, and each meeting and parting can start up a rollercoaster of insecurity. Wounds of rejection or abandonment can run deep and cause the bearer to build walls around their heart to protect it from pain. This card is a message that any walls you have around your heart will soon be shifting so you can dismantle them and begin to create the relationships you have always desired. Once the barriers soften and fall away, you will be able to hear the wisdom of your love language — the voice of your heart. These whispered blessings of support and acknowledgement will build your confidence and capacity to give and receive love. Relationships can be rich, passionate journeys into the profound truth of who you are. Through them, you can see yourself through another's eyes. They can reveal areas of yourself that you can embrace or heal. Vulnerability is not a weakness. The more you let people in, the stronger you can become — regardless of the outcome. In time, trust may be broken or strengthened. Either way, intimate relationships can heighten your experience of life. It is all part of the learning process. Relax, you are discovering the type of relationship you desire with yourself and others. Let love in!

Shadow Mastery Class: Experience Inner Intimacy

Meditation

Place a hand on the card. Gently close your eyes. Sense your body and concentrate on your breathing. Follow your breath inward. Hold for five seconds and relax. Breathe out and release all tension. Focus on the middle of your chest.

In front of you, a golden staircase descends into the earth. Relax as you walk down the ten healing steps to a magical, amethyst crystal cave. With each step, you become more deeply immersed in the qualities of unconditional love.

Step into the amethyst cave and greet your shadow. In front of you is an ornate door with 'Relationship Healing' written in emerald-green lettering. Bring to mind a relationship you want to heal. It could be any relationship — with a friend, family member, work colleague or romantic interest. The door opens, and you enter. The room is filled with emerald light and has two chairs. Sit in one and imagine the other person sitting in the other.

See and feel the emerald light flowing between you, linking your hearts. Thank the person for the opportunity to clear any challenging energy created by the outdated belief that love equals pain. The logical mind will tell you this is not true. You know that love will set you free on a deeper level. However, beliefs held within the shadow can override logic.

Gently set a new belief by affirming, "I am enough, I am worthy, I am love and I am loved." Breathe in and be filled with emerald light. Then send it to the other person and receive it from them. Feel the love healing and melting all walls that hold you away from love. Stay here for as long as you like — at least thirty seconds.

Thank and farewell the other person and see them gently fade from view. Stand up and move out of the room into the amethyst cave. Move to the golden staircase. As you walk upward, vow to live with an open heart, ready to receive love and express your desires. Allow passion, softness and generosity of spirit to fill you. Thank your shadow for caring for your intimacy. At the top of the stairs, take two deep breaths and open your eyes to love.

Inspired Insights, Reflections and Actions
- Meditating on the intention of being more intimate with your soul will uncover the truth that you are worthy of love and are safe to speak your truth.
- Acknowledge that how you see yourself may differ from how others see you. Ask three people what they like or love about you and do the same for them.
- Whenever you interact with anyone, you are in a relationship with them. Think about how you want your interactions to play out.

- The quality of your relationships becomes the quality of your life. Become clear about the type of people you want in your life.

Journal Work

Write down or draw a list of social values that are important to you, such as kindness, responsiveness, truthfulness, responsibility or self-respect. Next to each value, write down the feelings they evoke in you.

Next time you meditate, become aware of the way your values feel. Then take the feeling as far as you can into your day. Practise taking how you want to feel a little further into each day. The momentum of intention will grow these values in your interactions.

35. GRIEF

Opening a Natural Path to Healing Loss

Grief can be a whole-person experience that flows through body, mind and heart. This card has arrived to support and bring understanding to your grieving process. Loss can be met with shock or even denial, and emotions may fluctuate between rage and guilt. Then in its own time, acceptance gently embraces you. Healing begins as you discover a new perspective through all the twists and turns that open the light of day to the other side of grief. You begin to feel lighter and more resilient and realise that your soul's sweetness spilled through the cracks in your heart. Despite the pain of grief, your soul wants you to know how much you are loved, and your heart is more robust than you believe. When ready, it will work with you to heal and transform loss into liberation, bringing forth your strengths and renewed ways to assist yourself and others through grief.

Shadow Mastery Class: Finding a Soft Place to Land

Meditation

Place a hand on the card. Gently close your eyes. Sense your body and concentrate on your breathing. Follow your breath inward. Hold for five seconds and relax. Breathe out and release all tension. Focus on the middle of your chest.

In front of you, a golden staircase descends into the earth. Relax as you walk down the ten healing steps to a magical, amethyst crystal cave. Each step aligns you with your eternal and infinite higher self.

Step into the amethyst cave and greet your shadow. In front of you is a doorway with the word 'Relief' written above it. You walk through the opening and immediately feel better — softer, calmer and peaceful. You are standing on the beach of a beautiful tropical island. Gaze out over the ocean as you listen to the waves. Take in the colour and beauty of this wonderful place. It is a gorgeous day and the perfect temperature with the sun high in the sky. Feel the sun's rays gently warm you from head to toe, like liquid silk flowing over and within you — soothing, healing liquid gold.

Take off your shoes and feel the warm white sand tickle your feet as you scrunch your toes. Walk to the edge of the clear, stunning, turquoise-blue water. As you step into the water, the wet sand caresses your feet. The water is warm and soothing. Focus your gaze on the horizon and think of all the possibilities ahead for you, of all the wonderful things you would like to see, do and experience.

You see a hammock strung between two palm trees. Walk to it and climb in. You melt into this comfortable hammock and gently rock. This is a unique healing hammock that will soothe your heartache. As you lie here, warm golden light with remarkable healing properties from the heart of the Universe flows to you and bathes you. You don't need to do anything, just relax and allow this to happen. Stay here for as long as you like — at least thirty seconds.

When you are ready, float back through the doorway of relief with ease and take yourself to the golden staircase. As you ascend, allow softness and love to fill you. Thank your shadow for its gift of grief.

At the top of the stairs, take two deep breaths, then open your eyes. Be fully present in the beauty of you.

Inspired Insights, Reflections and Actions

Tears can represent a wall, a blockage or a pain dissolving within you. They can wash away the old so you can see through clear eyes.

Things to consider and try:

- Meet yourself where you are. Go easy on yourself, grieve for what has passed and let the pain be. Once you let all be as it is, you will begin to feel lighter. Healing has already started, and in the days that follow, inspired action will come to you.
- Immerse yourself in water and soak in its healing qualities. Take a bath or a shower, go for a swim or envision being embraced by cleansing, healing water. You might like to imagine your favourite colour flowing through the water.

Journal Work

To help you move through grief, write or draw about one challenging experience from your life. Ask yourself these questions as you are writing or drawing:

- Are you denying any aspects of the experience?
- How do you feel when you think about it? Once you write down a feeling, say, "Yes, I feel that way. What else do I feel?" Repeat until you have a list of at least five emotions.
- Is there anything you wish you had done differently?
- How have you accepted the loss and readjusted your life to it?

36. TRANSCEND

Beyond What You Think You Know

All the information that exists has always existed. In some ways, there is nothing new to teach or to learn. However, in the physical world, we can combine this information in different ways to create something new. Nobody has ever experienced this world the way you are. You are unique, continuously creating through expanding levels of interconnectedness that reveal new planes of existence and awareness. You are an innovator. Your consciousness filters your view of the world and influences your actions. The more heightened your consciousness, the broader and clearer your awareness and understanding. You are moving from learning into wisdom. Thank all you have experienced for giving you a choice to stay or move beyond. The freedom to transcend is yours.

Shadow Mastery Class: Expanding into You

Meditation

Place a hand on the card. Gently close your eyes. Sense your body and concentrate on your breathing. Follow your breath inward. Hold for five seconds and relax. Breathe out and release all tension. Focus on the middle of your chest.

In front of you, a golden staircase descends into the earth. Relax as you walk down the ten healing steps to a magical, amethyst crystal cave. Each step drops you into a deeper understanding of yourself. Greet your shadow.

A sphere of light gently oscillates back and forth in the middle of the cave. It draws you forwards into its light. You feel so calm and loved as you float through the translucent walls and find yourself floating above a three-dimensional flower of life with a seed at its centre. You have activated the seed just by being here. Watch in amazement as it breaks open to reveal a flower bud. Your flower begins to unfold one petal at a time. As it does so, your intuition and consciousness expand to embody the brilliance of your inner being. Outdated beliefs and restrictions are released, and a lightness of being pours through you.

Welcome your flower — then welcome its embrace as you journey deeper within your mystery. Within the flower, you float among delicate clouds of opalescent and iridescent colours above a landscape of great beauty and endless wonder. You are free to discover the riches of yourself. Stay here for as long as you like — at least thirty seconds.

As you leave the embrace of your flower of life, notice the fractals and sacred geometry being created. Return to the amethyst cave and the golden staircase. As you ascend, thank the darkness for revealing the difference between knowing the path and walking the path. With this revelation, you enter a mindset where everything becomes a way for you to transcend the mundane and know your truth. At the top of the stairs, take two deep breaths and open your sparkling, transcendent eyes.

Inspired Insights, Reflections and Actions

When you transcend outdated beliefs or perceptions, it is like closing unneeded apps and programs that take up valuable space and resources in your operating system. As your consciousness expands, you will see yourself from an elevated perspective and become more self-realised. You will notice patterns in how you approach your choices and the actions you take. It is also easier to see patterns in others.

Something to consider:

If there are things you don't like, start changing them. If you can't change them, walk away. If you can't walk away, elevate your perspective and connect with higher love. Perhaps, also make a plan for the future when you can make a change. Don't use those things as a reason not to feel loved or to feel disempowered.

Journal Work

Write or draw about a significant event, good or bad, from the last ten years. Knowing what you know now, would you approach that event differently? Compare what you want to achieve now with what you wanted to achieve then. Have your values and beliefs shifted? Has anything significant about you changed? In what ways would you like to grow and blossom in the future?

37. ANGER

Restoring Boundaries, Reclaiming Balance

Loudly defiant, simperingly silent, petulantly petty. Anger can manifest in our bodies, minds and hearts in many ways — so much so that the bearer may not recognise when their reactions, motivations and feelings are rising from anger. A situation may be causing you frustration right now. Tune in to your reactions and consider what they are telling you. Your sense of security and fairness may have been shaken, and it is okay to be angry. However, your reactions shape your world, so moving your anger out of the shadows can lead to expansion. Anger can reveal lifelong patterns that limit your growth. It may be easy to blame others for our anger, but in doing so, our own needs remain unexplored and disregarded. Waiting for someone or something out of your control to change so that you can stop being angry is futile. Your anger is your business, so ask it what it wants. From there, you can determine a course of action. Whatever it is fuelled by, you can choose to recognise or deny anger. Fighting it often causes it to push back and you can become more frustrated. Acknowledge and listen to your anger, and watch it transform into acceptance or action. Choose to make anger part of your empowerment process.

SHADOW MASTERY CLASS:
EMBRACE AND TRANSFORM ANGER INTO WISDOM

Meditation

Place a hand on the card. Gently close your eyes. Sense your body and concentrate on your breathing. Follow your breath inward. Hold for five seconds and relax. Breathe out and release all tension. Focus on the middle of your chest.

In front of you, a golden staircase descends into the earth. Relax as you walk down the ten healing steps to a magical, amethyst crystal cave. Each step immerses you deeper into the origins of your anger.

Step into the amethyst cave and greet your shadow. In front of you is a red door with the word 'Anger' etched upon it in gold. As you step through the door, you are bathed in the red light that fills the room. Instinctively, you know to sit in the chair in the middle of the room. It is so comfortable. Close your eyes. The feeling of anger moves around you. Let it be there. It has an important message to share:

Welcome, brave one. I am here to help you solve a problem. Get to know how I feel, so you can recognise me early before I feel the need to take over. I can be activated by stress or danger. In mild bursts, I can alert and protect you from perceived or real threats. However, when you don't acknowledge me or you cannot find a way to feel safe, I can start to overshadow other emotions. When I remain ignored and unaddressed, I will flow from your mind and into your body. You may feel your heart pounding, your shoulders tighten and your jaw clench. You may feel resentful, irritable, bitter or jealous or want to lash out. When this happens, sit and talk with me. Remember, I am here to help!

Bring to mind a situation or person that makes you angry. As you think about it, let anger begin to rise. Now, breathe deeply five times. Breathe into the waves of anger. Now, you are breathing in healing red light, which begins to dissipate and calm it. Unclench your jaw and your hands, and drop your shoulders. Take five more long, deep red breaths, and be open to the message about what prompted your anger to come forth. Stay here for as long as you like — at least thirty seconds.

Leave the red room and return to the amethyst cave. Walk to the golden staircase. As you ascend, notice that you feel light and calm. Thank your shadow for holding the fuel of anger when you didn't know what to do with it. At the top of the stairs, take two deep breaths in and out and open your eyes to absolute relief.

Inspired Insights, Reflections and Actions

Anger is filled with energy that can be harnessed and used to create change and cleanse the shadow. However, if it is denied or becomes a habit, it loses its power and becomes an obstacle to growth. Anger feels dynamic and active, which gives the impression of moving forwards, but it could be masking another issue.

When you feel angry, try sitting with it. Breathe into it and let it just be. Count to ten and take note of how you feel. Listen to what is beneath the anger. Repeat until the anger has transformed or dissipated.

Journal Work

Write about or draw your anger. How does it feel? What part of you do you think it comes from? What does it look like? What does it have to tell you? Who makes you angry and why?

Explore your anger. Get to know it so you can understand it more clearly and respond to it in ways that open your heart and mind to solutions.

38. DREAM WORK

Messages from the Unconscious

Your dream world is communicating with you, not with words but with vibrations. When you recall a dream, you translate the vibes into pictures and sound with a narrative. Dreams are an incredible insight into your soul truth, whether nocturnal or waking dreams. Different types of dreams offer their own benefits. Pleasant or wish-fulfilment dreams soften your resistance to positive outcomes. What you experience in your dreams feels more possible in reality. Recurring dreams repeat themselves with minor variations because something remains unresolved in your life. A resolution will bring them to an end. Prophetic dreams tap into the vibrational world that precedes the physical. Nightmares can be any or a combination of these dreams and be a response to buried trauma or ignored situations. They alert you to thought patterns or beliefs that hold you in fear and are a chance to face your worries. In daydreams and lucid dreams, you are aware that you are dreaming. Both enable the dreamer to be an active participant. Taking control of your dreams by flying away from a threat or leaping beyond an obstacle can turn nightmares into welcome adventures. This can have tremendous real-world benefits. Pay attention to your dreams, and they will reveal even more insight!

Shadow Mastery Class: Actualise a Dream

Meditation

Place a hand on the card. Gently close your eyes. Sense your body and concentrate on your breathing. Follow your breath inward. Hold for five seconds and relax. Breathe out and release all tension. Focus on the middle of your chest.

A golden staircase that descends into the earth materialises in front of you. As you walk down the ten healing steps to a magical, amethyst crystal cave, bring to mind a nightmare or dream for clarification. Step into the amethyst cave and greet your shadow. A magical dream portal appears before you. Take your dream with you as you step into the portal.

You land in the middle of your dream. Know that this is your place, and you control it. Think about what you want to happen, and it will. You can dive deeper or pull back from your dream at any time. Through your mind's eye, you can see everything in all directions. Allow the vision to unfold around you. Enjoy this empowering exercise to gain more excellent knowledge about your soul wisdom. Reflect on your feelings during the dream. What symbols or images jump out at you? What waking emotions and events can you see or feel? Realise that each aspect of the dream represents an aspect of you.

As the dream unfolds, it shows you aspects you were previously unaware of: the underlying belief that is driving the dream pattern and the reason this dream is so important. Breathe in and be filled with the wonderment of your dream, and let it share messages with you. Stay here for as long as you like — at least thirty seconds.

Move through the dream portal into the amethyst cave. Return to the golden staircase. As you ascend, summarise how you will implement the answers you just received. Thank your shadow for being a part of your dream world.

At the top of the stairs, take two deep breaths and open your eyes to all possibilities.

Inspired Insights, Reflections and Actions
Things to consider:

- When you sleep, you move into complete alignment with yourself, into a state of oneness where no resistance exists — so all is possible.
- Dreams are energetic conversations and experiences that help give meaning and knowing to your life.
- Recalling a dream is a physical translation of the energetic clouds of thought and knowing that are drawn to you.

Journal Work

Make a space in your journal for dream work or have a separate dream journal. Place it next to your bed with a pen or pencil. You can also use your phone or another electronic device.

Before you sleep, say to yourself, "My intention tonight is to sleep well so I wake up completely refreshed and renewed. If something important happens in my dream time, I will recall it easily."

Before you get up, as you lie in a beautiful fresh state of being awake, breathe gently for a few minutes. What dreams do you remember? If a dream comes forwards, relax and think about how you felt during the dream. The way you feel about it will give you more information than if you interpret the details. This is actualising rather than interpreting your dream.

If you awaken from a nightmare, take a few breaths and let any fear pass. Rather than worry or distress, allow your body, mind and heart to calm and feel appreciation for the message. The dream may be informing you of something unwanted, where you have barriers to your desires.

39. PROJECTION

The World as Your Emotional Canvas

Unacknowledged hurts from your shadow can be placed upon and attributed to someone or something. This is an unconscious way to protect yourself from inner conflict and worry. You may not be ready to process how you feel. However, your mind needs a perspective to help it understand a challenging event. So, projection can occur without you realising it as a way to recognise and heal a hurt stored deep in your shadow. When something is in the shadows, it can't be seen, but it goes everywhere with you. You begin to see this aspect of your shadow world reflected in the world around you. When you understand that everything can teach you something about yourself, you can assess whether your uncomfortable feelings about someone or something highlight an unresolved personal hurt. Allow these feelings to inspire curiosity and wonder and create integrating and healing paths to your desires.

Shadow Mastery Class: The Projection Room

Meditation

Place a hand on the card. Gently close your eyes. Sense your body and concentrate on your breathing. Follow your breath inward. Hold for five seconds and relax. Breathe out and release all tension. Focus on the middle of your chest.

In front of you, a golden staircase descends into the earth. Relax as you walk down the ten healing steps to a magical, amethyst crystal cave. With each step, you realise that what you see in the world is a facet of you. Step into the amethyst cave and greet your shadow.

In front of you is a red velvet curtain. When you touch it, you realise it is made of light. The curtains open, and you walk through into your projection room. This is your very own movie theatre. You are about to watch a beautifully crafted scene to help you understand projection. Take a seat on a comfortable, warm, soft chair.

The scene begins. Two people meet. One has unfairly criticised the other. The person unjustly treated places all hurt, criticism and judgement into a basket. They then hand the basket to the other person while saying, "I can see you are hurting, but these belong to you. It is time to face and own your pain so you can love yourself more wholly."

The other person takes the basket and says, "Thank you for

returning what belongs to me. I am sorry for placing my hurt on you. With this basket, you have given me the courage to process and integrate the wisdom from my pain."

As you observe this scene, think about scenarios when you have played either of these parts. Observe your findings without judgement. You will begin to understand how pain and hurt open a pathway to your soul truth so that you can inspire yourself and others. Take all the time you need to peruse the information you have just received.

When you feel ready, move through the red velvet curtain of light into the amethyst cave. Return to the golden staircase. As you walk upward, know that you can reimagine and recreate anything in your mind and life. Thank your shadow for projecting your hurt and admiration into the world so you can see them with clarity. At the top of the stairs, take two deep breaths and open your eyes to the magic of possibility.

Inspired Insights, Reflections and Actions
Projection works both ways. The beautiful things you see in others are aspects of yourself that you have not yet integrated. We can more easily recognise something in another when we have that quality in ourselves.

Consider the following:

- When you react positively or negatively when watching a movie, check in with yourself. What do you think it is telling you?
- Become aware of other people projecting their stuff onto you so you don't doubt yourself.

Journal Work

Use the world as your mirror. Write or draw what you observe about yourself.

40. JUDGEMENT

*When All Sides are Equal,
the Path of Liberated Wisdom Appears*

Someone's behaviour, mannerisms or presence may have become a source of irritation. Look within. You might have asked them to change the behaviour, or they may have sensed your subtle disapproval and even tried to accommodate you. When the prickly feeling remains, it is time to go inward. It is easy to judge or diminish someone or something without exploring why these feelings have arisen. Like all feelings, judgement, irritation and criticism are signposts for you. Following them may be uncomfortable and, perhaps, reveal something you secretly judge about yourself. It can be confronting when your inner critic comes out to play and judge you. Breathe and relax. You have done nothing wrong and are not being punished. Listen to your inner critic — observe how it speaks, the phrases it uses and any words it emphasises. These are all clues on your journey of self-discovery. When you feel judgement arise, breathe and relax. It is a stress response. Detach and observe your judgement and let it float away, taking a layer of conditioning with it. As those layers lift, your soul truth will begin to reveal itself more clearly. When judgement turns up, be gentle, be still and let it show the path to liberation.

Shadow Mastery Class: Meet Your Inner Critic

Meditation

Place a hand on the card. Gently close your eyes. Sense your body and concentrate on your breathing. Follow your breath inward. Hold for five seconds and relax. Breathe out and release all tension. Focus on the middle of your chest.

In front of you, a golden staircase descends into the earth. Walk down the ten healing steps to a magical, amethyst crystal cave. As you move down the steps, allow any unbalanced beliefs to rise gently. When you arrive at the bottom, step into the amethyst cave and greet your shadow.

A dirty, old wooden door looms in front of you. The words 'Inner Critic' are carved into it. It feels intimidating, but you are ready to face this part of yourself. Open the door and step through into a dark and musty room. The space feels sad and tired. A silhouette is huddled in the corner. You walk over and place a hand on their shoulder.

The person turns around — it is you, a sad, scared, tired

version of you. This surprises you. It is not some sort of monster or ghost of someone with authority. No, your inner critic is you. They look back at you and say:

Finally, you have come to love me. That is all I want. I have never felt lovable. I have been pointing out all our flaws so you could fix them, then accept, love, hug me and make me part of your life.

Gift yourself a moment of silence to process this message. You may have blamed your inner critic for being so harsh. But just like you, it wants to be accepted and loved. Gift them that acceptance now. Thank them for trying to keep you safe from others' judgement. Let it know you are happy and healing who you are and no longer need an inner critic. It is now being promoted to inner equaliser. Its job is to identify areas of imbalance and offer ways to rebalance your energy. The figure is transformed by its newfound purpose, and joy flows through you both as you embrace. Stay here for as long as you like — at least thirty seconds.

The room is now light, bright and full of loving energy. You and your inner critic have become one. This room has become a temple you can visit when you wish to rebalance.

Step into the amethyst cave and walk to the golden staircase. As you ascend, you feel lovable. Thank the darkness for giving your inner critic a voice. At the top of the stairs, take two deep breaths and open your eyes of love.

Inspired Insights, Reflections and Actions

Your inner critic comprises conditioned thoughts picked up through life as ways to fit in, be loved or be accepted. Healthy judgement is a way of assessing information to gain a balanced perspective before making a decision. Unhealthy judgement might try to justify unbalanced beliefs.

Try this: Close your eyes to disengage from the stimulus of the outside world and reconnect with your soul truth. You have access to your values from this place of alignment, where the best course of action will come to you.

Journal Work
When your inner equaliser falls back into its role of critic, bring out your journal and describe them in words or pictures. What do they look like? What do they sound like? What colour and size are they? Become familiar with them so you can recognise them and remind them of their new purpose. When they are convinced you need a critic, not an equaliser, to keep you safe, and its voice gets too loud, give it a cookie (baked with love and acceptance) and direct it to a corner to eat it quietly.

41. SHADOW SONG

Hear Your Soul Song

Music is transformative. It can take you through and beyond present states of heart and mind and connect you with memories, feelings, hopes and dreams. The music you play when you are sad or despondent provides a pathway for your shadow to work with your consciousness to help you find balance and healing. Music bypasses the mind and penetrates the heart so you can free emotion. It may feel uncomfortable, raw or chaotic at first. However, music gifts you a safe way to be with and explore feelings so you can become comfortable with them, and healing can begin. When a song connects you with hurt or bad memories, it may be your shadow communicating with you. It shows you how to hear your soul song and live your full potential. All music has its purpose. Diverse genres and vibes allow us to face and release different levels of emotion — from despair and anger to joy and ecstasy.

Shadow Mastery Class:
Listening to the Soundtrack of Your Life

Meditation

Before you begin, play a melancholy playlist or song on repeat at a low volume.

Place a hand on the card. Gently close your eyes. Sense your body and concentrate on your breathing. Follow your breath inward. Hold for five seconds and relax. Breathe out and release all tension. Then focus on the middle of your chest.

In front of you, a golden staircase descends into the earth. Walk down the ten healing steps to a magical, amethyst crystal cave. Each step reveals a deeper level of sadness. Step into the amethyst cave and greet your shadow. In front of you is a door labelled 'Shadow Song Room'. Open the door and enter the room.

All you hear in the dimly lit room is your breathing and heartbeat. You notice a disc spinning and floating in the space. It begins to play a song. Against the blackness of the room, colour emerges from the disc. You are seeing the vibrations of sound. The colours become streamers and ribbons which move around you in a dance of wild freedom. You too can join the dance. The music sounds richer and nebulous clouds of light join the symphony of colour within the room. Open your heart and mind to the full experience of the music as you breathe light and sound into your body. Let it all in — all you can and can't sense. Imagine you and the music becoming one in an energetic dance.

Feel the entirety of you — the wondermert, the wisdom and your soul song. Let the music bypass any walls and beliefs you put up to keep your emotions safe. Be present in the magnificence of you and your symphony of feeling. Allow the wisdom of your soul song to rise and dance within and around you. Stay here for as long as you like — at least thirty seconds.

When you are ready, float out of the room into the amethyst cave on a wave of sound that takes you to the golden staircase. As you gently float up the stairs, you vow to hear and listen to the soundtrack of your life with an open heart. Thank your shadow for communicating in this way. At the top of the stairs, take two deep breaths and open your eyes to new ways of interacting with music.

Inspired Insights, Reflections and Actions
When a song moves you to tears, your shadow may be helping you find balance.

Try this: Put on a song you listen to when you are sad. Really listen to the words, then ask yourself, "What is this helping me to understand and heal?"

Listen to recorded music or meditations that contain binaural beats, solfeggio frequencies or brainwave entrainment. Record how you feel.

Journal Work
Write down three movies or songs that bring you to tears and connect with your heart. Then write down or draw the sensations, emotions and messages you take from them. You are sensing and being alerted to the shadow song that will lead to your soul song.

42. INTEGRITY

Loyalty to Innermost Truth

In the quiet moments, when there are no distractions, and we have only ourselves for company, honest feelings, reflections, hopes and fears can stir into consciousness. Any unease or worry that you may have been ignoring can suddenly become loud and present. This card suggests you've been avoiding the quiet moments, as there is a self-truth you aren't keen on tackling. Take a breath and draw on your courage — it's time to have an honest conversation with yourself so you can be free from this energy-zapping avoidance. Integrity is not just about you — when you lie to yourself, you lie to others. When you aren't honest with yourself, can you expect others to be honest with you? Have you promised yourself you would (or wouldn't) do something but let yourself down? If someone else continually broke their word, you would stop trusting them. Perhaps you are avoiding yourself as you feel unsettled, guilty or disappointed that you haven't achieved, overcome, completed or committed to something you had set your mind on. Be gentle with yourself. It's okay. Instead of making promises that can perpetuate self-doubt and diminish your faith in yourself, listen to and support your whole self. Honour your word to love and cherish your past, present and future selves, and your integrity will strengthen naturally.

Shadow Mastery Class: Honour Your Honesty

Meditation

Place a hand on the card. Gently close your eyes. Sense your body and concentrate on your breathing. Follow your breath inward. Hold for five seconds and relax. Breathe out and release all tension. Focus on the middle of your chest.

In front of you, a golden staircase descends into the earth. Walk down the ten healing steps to a magical, amethyst crystal cave. As you move down the steps, allow untruths to gently rise to be healed and released. When you arrive at the bottom, step into the magical, crystal amethyst cave and greet your shadow.

A wooden door with a crack running through it appears in front of you. The words 'Seeing Truth Through the Gap' are written on it. The crack becomes larger and larger until you can walk through it into a round room bathed in soft blue light. The room feels familiar and comforting.

The room goes dark. You continue to feel safe and secure. Listen with your senses. Nothing happens at first, and then you hear a faint whisper, a familiar voice, "Feel your way through, have faith in the whispers of your soul."

A large lapis lazuli rises in the centre of the room. Blue and gold light shines from within the crystal. It illuminates your truth. It is beautiful and mesmerising. Breathe in the blue and gold and allow messages to flow to you.

Your throat chakra enables you to communicate with truth, wisdom and confidence. Notice the health of your throat. Is there darkness or brightness there? Ask your throat to show you where you may not be expressing your needs, feelings and desires with yourself and others.

It is time to choose love over fear. Become the blue and the gold light and see yourself happily expressing your uniqueness in any way that brings you joy. Stay here for as long as you like — at least thirty seconds.

Notice a letter on the lapis lazuli. It is from your soul and will reveal your higher communications. Open it and read the cosmic message that is just for you today, then place the letter in your pocket and leave the room through the gap in the door.

Step into the amethyst cave and walk to the golden staircase. As you ascend, you become truth, wisdom and love. Thank the darkness for illuminating the integrity of your soul light. At the top of the stairs, take two deep breaths and open your eyes of honesty.

Inspired Insights, Reflections and Actions
When your mind, heart and soul are in agreement, you will feel energised by integrity. This is your wise truth.

Consider and try the following:

- Commit to something only when you know you will do it. If you are unsure about something, be truthful to yourself and others. For example, "I'm not ready yet, but I will be soon." Or, "I would love to help you, but I can't at the moment. Who else can we get to help you?"
- You are the custodian of your soul. As you nurture your mind and heart, your soul's integrity will be easier to hear. It will always feel loving and feed your values.

Journal Work

For 24 hours, anytime you criticise or judge yourself, say, "Harmony" (or a word that resonates with your soul integrity). Then, write down or draw a compliment or an affirmation of support. Take note of any recurring themes and write an affirming mantra that you can repeat morning and night that specifically addresses it. You and your soul are co-creating words of power that support your integrity.

43. INTEGRATION

Ushering Experience into Wisdom

You are beginning to see the benefits of your life experiences, the good and the bad, and how they intersect to create a rich platform from which to build. When you can appreciate the lessons and strengths developed through adversity, the challenging aspects of your reality can transform into wisdom. In this way, they no longer limit but expand your world and your potential. Gratitude doesn't absolve wrongdoing. Instead, it allows you to move forwards with balanced awareness. Rather than feeling that anything has control over your reactions, you can choose your responses. Blaming an experience or person for how you feel gives them influence that can colour your life. Turn towards your shadow self and look at anything or anyone you have made responsible for how you feel. Face them with honesty and courage. Tell them you are your own person, that you are strong and in command of your choices and feelings. Thank yourself for bravely claiming power and wisdom from adversity. Know that you are whole and free to be all you are.

Shadow Mastery Class: Embracing the Whole Package

Meditation

Have the whole card deck with you when you begin, as you will need it to answer a question and work on topics from other cards during your meditation.

Place a hand on the Integration card. Close your eyes. Sense your body and concentrate on your breathing. Follow your breath inward. Hold for five seconds and relax. Breathe out and release all tension. Focus on the middle of your chest.

In front of you, a golden staircase descends into the earth. Relax as you walk down the ten healing steps to a magical, amethyst crystal cave. Each step blends into the next with integrating harmony.

At the bottom of the steps, greet your shadow, then sit in the middle of the cave. Ask, "Where can I benefit from residual healing?"

When you feel ready, open your eyes, take the rest of the deck and shuffle for as long as you need. Fan out the cards and choose one. This card reveals an area where you have not entirely integrated the wisdom of a challenging event. The remaining hurt has become so familiar that it seems inconsequential, almost invisible. Do that card's meditation from being in the amethyst cave (as you are already there) until it says, "Stay here for as long as you like."

You are doing fantastic work.

Now, find a comfortable place to lie down and stay here for as long as you like. Allow the energy of integration to show you the steps to take in your everyday life for even higher dimensions of growth and expansion.

When you feel ready, return to the golden staircase. As you ascend, let integration be your new normal. Walk through life without pulling anything towards you or pushing it away. Your circumstances will inspire your next steps. Thank your shadow for holding all the disowned parts until you were ready to include them. At the top of the stairs, take two deep breaths and open your loving, accepting eyes.

Inspired Insights, Reflections and Actions
'Integration' comes from the Latin word *integratus*, meaning "to make whole." To integrate an experience or inner quality is to take responsibility for it rather than rejecting, denying or pushing it away, which will cause separation. When you integrate your shadow, it no longer acts out of the darkness. It becomes a part of the whole and transforms into light and heart love.

Try making a different dish or taking a cooking class. Bringing ingredients together to create something new and yummy will help you with your integration process.

Journal Work
Bring to mind an experience or feeling you want to shift, heal or move through. Write, draw, paint, dance, cry, smile, build or breathe your way through it. Each experience, emotion and person is unique — honour what feels right for you and the situation. Record your conclusions in your journal.

44. RESILIENCE

Centred Through Harmony and Chaos

You are creating an empowered, resilient self by gradually replacing limiting thinking with a focus on strength, growth and love. Move beyond what others think to a place where you have so much faith in your reality that you can stand alone without feeling lonely. Personal power and resilience exist in every cell of your body. Be still and listen to yourself. Let those who rush around trying to action everything do their thing. When they speak, listen and assess. When they push forwards, patiently watch and evaluate before acting. When they panic, still your heart and offer resilience and strength. When you see people who need help, be centred in your courage and conviction and act accordingly. Congratulations, you are becoming spiritually fitter.

Shadow Mastery Class: Discover Your Grit

Meditation

Before beginning this meditation, you may like to familiarise yourself with your spiritual warrior (see Card 10). Place a hand on the card. Gently close your eyes. Sense your body and concentrate on your breathing. Follow your breath inward. Hold for five seconds and relax. Breathe out and release all tension. Focus on the middle of your chest.

In front of you, a golden staircase descends into the earth. As you walk down to the magical amethyst cave, feel your mind and body focus entirely on each of the ten healing steps. Each step opens your mind to your wisdom.

Step into the amethyst cave and greet your shadow. A massive wooden door bursts open, and your spiritual warrior welcomes you. They take you by the hand and lead you through the door, saying, "You are ready." A mixture of curiosity and fear fills you, but you also feel that this is something special.

Your warrior leads you to the banks of a river so vast that it looks like an inland sea. You sit down together, and your warrior places one hand on your heart and the other at your third eye, between your eyebrows. You feel your warrior's energy merging with yours, and information begins to pour into you:

> *This is the warrior's way. Persist with willpower and mindfulness to control and direct your thoughts and emotions. Honour your body with a growth mindset, focus on your strengths and learn from your patterns. Stay curious and passionate and follow your creative passion without the need for external motivation.*

Master your inner world, replace negativity with positivity and cultivate gratitude. Face your fears and train your weaknesses. Know your strengths, but work on your weaknesses until they are no longer weak. Embrace life and stop focusing on the weeds. Fill your garden with flowers. When things go wrong, be your best self. Be adaptable, flexible and open to new solutions. Honour yourself, all sentient beings and nature. You are a warrior.

Integrate with the way of the warrior as it inspires images, feelings and symbols to come to you. Stay here for as long as you like — at least thirty seconds.

Your warrior asks you to stand, and you both return to the door in silence. Love and compassion for your warrior fills you. They send you through the door into the amethyst cave, saying, "It's up to you now!"

Walk to the golden staircase. As you ascend, you feel inspired to implement the way of the warrior in your everyday life. When circumstances knock you off-centre, your resilience will bring you back to your heart and warrior wisdom.

Thank the darkness for accommodating your warrior. Take a big breath and open your eyes to the master that you are.

Inspired Insights, Reflections and Actions

The way of the warrior cultivates complete trust in inner wisdom, so you can find the advantage of whatever you are experiencing — good or bad.

Consider the following:

- Try adjusting and adapting to situations you are not comfortable with. Aim to be more resilient and not take things personally.
- Try a martial art — t'ai chi, aikido, karate, taekwondo, jujutsu or judo, for example.

Journal Work

Ask two people you know to write down three of your weaknesses. Tell them it is for this exercise, that you won't take it personally and that it is to support your growth mindset. Read what they have written when you return to your journal. Write down or draw your response.

Do this exercise when you feel relaxed and confident that you can be objective and compassionate about what is written. If you do feel upset or confronted by what is written, write about or draw your feelings in your journal. Thank your friends for their honesty.

45. FULFILMENT

Striking Gold in Every Experience

You have stepped out of a shadow into a dream or desire. You have self-actualised and shifted your reality into a new kind of normal. It's time to get ready for contrasting experiences that will inspire bigger dreams and desires! Fulfilment is the ability to feel joyous satisfaction with your manifested desires, knowing they create the foundations for fresh desires to arise. The fundamental nature of growth is change. The Universe expands into greater understanding for the sheer joy of experiencing creation — as do you. Fresh desires are rising within you. Define them and allow them to blossom. Enjoying every part of the realisation process, including this moment, is a secret of deliberate creation. You are constantly fulfilled.

Shadow Mastery Class: Creating Gold from Lead

Meditation

Place a hand on the card. Gently close your eyes. Sense your body and concentrate on your breathing. Follow your breath inward. Hold for five seconds and relax. Breathe out and release all tension. Then focus on the middle of your chest.

In front of you, a golden staircase descends into the earth. Relax as you walk down the ten healing steps into a magical amethyst cave. Each step immerses you in the qualities of golden fulfilment. When you arrive at the crystal cave, find a comfortable place to sit. Greet your shadow and thank it for all it has done for you.

Golden, red and blue light begins to pour into the cave. These rays bathe you in feelings of fulfilment and satisfaction. Imagine inhaling the colours through your nose and exhaling through your mouth. Feel or see yourself radiate with the light of self-actualisation as you embrace all aspects of your shadow and bring it into your heart. Feel the alchemical transformation of darkness into light taking place in your heart. As you accept and integrate with your shadow, pink light shines from your unified heart as a celebration of love and wholeness. You are creating space for freedom, love, empowerment and creation.

You live in this world, unbound by anyone else's creations. You have set yourself free. You are a genius creator in this magnificent body that you created for the sole purpose of experiencing life in new and beautiful ways. You are an alchemist. What do you want your life to look and feel like? Be still, listen and stay here for as long as you like — at least thirty seconds.

Return to the golden staircase. As you ascend, know that your light will encourage others to discover theirs. By being and living your authentic soul life, you will become a beacon of freedom. Let golden love be with you as you return to your daily life. Thank the darkness for illuminating extraordinary ways to truly embrace every fragment of you. At the top of the stairs, take two deep breaths and open your eyes to your fulfilling life.

Inspired Insights, Reflections and Actions
Fulfilment is similar to the concept of enlightenment or self-actualisation. As the nature of life is to continually expand, these states are not permanently accomplished and held. Everything moves and changes, and so must you. Whatever brought you to this moment has passed. Focus on what you choose to do and feel from this moment onward.

Exercise: Research spiritual alchemy — the idea of turning your dross (fears, trauma, wounds or limiting belief systems) into gold (fulfilment, enlightenment, joy or bliss).

Journal Work
Write or draw a list of seven past dreams or desires that have arrived in your life, big or small. Thank yourself for fulfilling your dreams and desires. Thank your soul and all who were cooperative components in these creations.

Now, write or draw seven new dreams and desires. Every six months, check your list. If a dream has come true, add another dream or desire and keep your list of seven going. If you can draw or write it and believe it, you will create and experience it.

About the Author

DENISE JARVIE is a soul coach and mentor who reconnects people with their authenticity and soul vision to awaken broader life possibilities. She is open and warm, with a loving sense of humour that creates a safe space for any topic to be worked through. Denise's soul vision is to inspire kindness, curiosity and big dreams for the growth and enhancement of humanity, animals and nature.

Denise was not exposed to any education to understand and release difficult emotions as she grew up. So, she stored them inside and moved on — until they manifested as anxiety and depression. After a difficult time, she was motivated to change her career and look for lasting answers. This began 25 years of studying and practising meditation, metaphysics, psychology and healing.

Denise was born in the south of England, near Stonehenge. When she was three, her family immigrated to Melbourne, Australia, and she now lives in Sydney with her quirky Tonkinese cat. When she is not writing, coaching, or teaching, she loves cooking, gardening and working out.

Denise is the bestselling creator of *The Secret Language of Light Oracle*, *The Flower of Life*, *The Tarot of Light*, *11:11 Meditations*, *Dissolving Stress*, *Flower of Life Meditations* and *Mandala Healing Oracle*.

For more information on Denise and her visionary work, visit **www.denisejarvie.com**.

About the Artist

At a young age, Daniel B. Holeman had a profound spiritual awakening and experienced the nature of pure consciousness from which the manifest world is created. Since then, his life has been about deepening that awareness and sharing it with others through art, lifestyle, conversation and guidance.

Daniel is inspired to assist others aspiring to their unique purpose and gifts and living from that place — their fullest potential. He knows that more people being that way will bring about a better world for all. Daniel invites the viewer to dive into a deeper dimension of consciousness while gazing at his paintings.

Artistic talent combined with his lifelong exploration of consciousness and devotion to self-realisation has given Daniel the ability to depict inspiring and profound sacred imagery. Many have been touched by his work and describe it as profoundly moving and inspiring. Born and raised in San Jose, USA, Daniel currently resides in California, where he works on various projects.

For more information about Daniel's inspirational work, visit **www.AwakenVisions.com**.

ALSO AVAILABLE FROM BLUE ANGEL PUBLISHING®

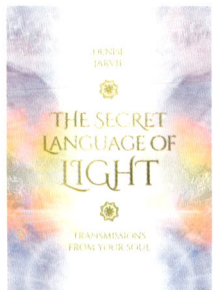

The Secret Language of Light
Transmissions from your Soul

Denise Jarvie
Artwork by Daniel B. Holeman

The impulse to create and energise peace, love and fulfilment is alive within you. This glorious oracle works with the mysteries and secrets of the light to illuminate the rich possibility and potential inside you. The light is a constant guide and support, and its language inspires, empowers and activates your soul spark.

Step into the wonder of the light through the inspired insight of Denise Jarvie and the radiant artwork of Daniel B. Holeman to enliven the love, vision and strength of your heart. Access the wisdom of these stunning cards through the specifically designed meditations, reflections, and exercises for divination, contemplation, or revelation. You can also work through the 45 cards and detailed 164-page guidebook for a complete soul mastery class. The language of light speaks to eternity, to life, and to you. Tune into its secrets and shine!

ISBN: 978-1-925538-47-2
45 cards and 164-page guidebook.

ALSO AVAILABLE FROM BLUE ANGEL PUBLISHING*

Mandala Healing Oracle
Journey to Your Heart

Denise Jarvie
Artwork by Lindy Longhurst

Follow your breath on a colour-filled journey into healing, magic and inspiration and awaken the strength, peace and vibrant creativity at your core. As you explore these beautiful mandalas from the outside in, you will delve into the hidden hues, rich imagery and glorious metaphor of your subconscious, your higher self and your innate potential.

Together, the delightful images, colour guide, messages, meditations and journal prompts will gently release stressors, so you move toward your dreams and desires with calm and confidence. Enhance intuition and self-understanding, and enjoy your daily adventure in the beautiful world where we live. Enjoy!

ISBN: 978-1-922573-09-4
44 circular cards and 140-page guidebook.

ALSO AVAILABLE FROM BLUE ANGEL PUBLISHING®

The Tarot of Light

Denise Jarvie
Artwork by Toni Carmine Salerno

Tarot is a path of self-knowing that unveils the mysteries that lie before and within us. The divine and loving messages within *The Tarot of Light* offer a balanced view of past, present and future, so your readings bring illumination, learning, insight, and direction for a brighter, lighter tomorrow.

Denise Jarvie brings a contemporary approach to traditional tarot that features seventy-eight of Toni Carmine Salerno's most enchanting artworks. The suits of the minor arcana have become Angels (Swords), Hearts (Cups), Stars (Wands), and Trees (Pentacles) to align with the themes that run through Toni's work. Denise also revisits the 22 cards of the major arcana, so they reflect modern-day archetypes. These cards hold divine and loving energy to encourage harmonious perceptions and help you manifest your hopes, dreams and desires. Don't just see the future, co-create it!

ISBN: 978-0-6487467-2-0
78 cards and 120-page guidebook.

ALSO AVAILABLE FROM BLUE ANGEL PUBLISHING®

The Flower of Life
Wisdom of Astar

Denise Jarvie

The Flower of Life contains the seed of all possibilities, the essence of all desire. This powerful creative symbol which lends its name to this deck and graces the back of each card within it holds infinite divine potential. These cards are a portal to connect you with that very potential locked deep within you. Take a journey with Astar, a wise, loving energetic consciousness whose energy permeates this deck with incredible wisdom and insights to share to help you remember your true beauty and worth. Here is a star map of your potential. Astar holds the faith of your love and truth even when you have forgotten and constantly streams it to you through the light of our day star – the Sun and the sparkling stars at night.

ISBN: 978-1-922161-26-0
52 guidance cards and booklet.

Notes

Notes

Notes

Notes

For more information on this
or any Blue Angel Publishing release,
please visit our website at:

www.BlueAngelOnline.com